Richard,

we hope you enjoy our Famous Book!

Sincerely,
Marc + Brian

Really Appreciate you Richard!

BECOMING
FAMOUS

The Associate Driven Culture That Fuels
A 4th-Generation Family Business

THE BLAUSHILD FAMILY
with Brooke Bates

SMART BUSINESS® BOOKS
An Imprint of Smart Business® Network Inc.

Becoming Famous
COPYRIGHT © 2019 The Blaushild Family

All rights are reserved.

No part of this publication may be reproduced, distributed or transmitted in any form or by any means, including photocopying, recording or other digital or mechanical methods, without the prior written permission of the author, except in the cases of fair use as permitted by U.S. and international copyright laws.
For permission requests, please submit in writing to the publisher at the address below:

Published by Smart Business Books
An imprint of Smart Business Network Inc.
835 Sharon Drive, Suite 200
Westlake, OH 44145

Printed in the United States of America
Editor: Dustin S. Klein

ISBN: 978-1-945389-87-0
Library of Congress Control Number: 9781945389870

CONTENTS

Foreword 9

Introduction 11

EARLY GROWTH

    Building Our Famous Culture 21

    Branching Out 25

    Empowered to Grow 31

FAMILY

    Family First 37

    The Call that Changed Everything 39

    Joining the Famous Family 43

    Growing Up in the Family Business 49

    Famous Family Fund 59

    Being in a Family Business 61

    Building a Legacy 65

TRUST

    Trust is Like a Field of Horses 71

    Taking Service Personally 75

    Be in the Gray Zone 79

    Learning from Mistakes 8

COMMUNICATION

Technology Transformation 89

Crystal Ball 95

The Third Generation 101

The Heart of the Operation 105

A Different Way of Communicating 109

Listening for Better Decisions 115

TEAMWORK

For the Common Good of the Team 121

Recruiting Team Players 125

The Sharing of Knowledge 129

Getting the Right People in the Right Roles 133

Teamwork in Tough Times 137

CONTINUOUS IMPROVEMENT

Celebrating 75 Years 143

Back to Basics 147

Famous University 151

Continuous Improvement Mindset 155

Moving Out of the Castle 159

Giving Back 161

No Conclusion 165

Foreword
by Marc Blaushild

It would be difficult to start this book without thanking the many people who made it possible. First, I'd like to thank our Famous Family. Our valued associates are the heart and soul of our company, and we've been fortunate to work and enjoy life with so many great people. There are far too many to name, and the relationships we have with our dedicated and loyal Associates, valued Customers and key Suppliers is what makes life so meaningful.

The opportunity to reflect and encapsulate what we've experienced during our time at Famous would not be possible without Brooke Bates. Brooke spent countless hours interviewing Famous Family members to create something special from their stories. Brooke, Dustin S. Klein, and the rest of the Smart Business team are the reason our story could take shape as a book.

To my incredible Vistage Group, our legal team at Sonkin & Koberna, our accounting team at Cohen & Company, our lender at PNC Bank, and past and present Advisory Board members Brad Roller, Rich Conti, Rick Sonkin, Brent Grover and Jay Greyson; your constant support, guidance and feedback keeps me and our team grounded and focused as we work to continuously improve.

We would not have the opportunity to grow without those who came before us. My father, Jay, and his father, Hyman, and their respective teams built the foundation of our business. Dad, everything you've done for the business, and taught me and others is what enables us to continue improving the business. Thank you.

As I look to the future, I feel so blessed to have two incredible sons. Brian and Kevin, you are both so caring, kind, smart, respectful and fun. Your desire to improve our business for the sake of our associates and customers is special, and none of us take that for granted. I learn from you as much as I hope you both learn from me. Kevin, your tireless work, perseverance and attention to detail with our editors brought this book to completion.

Last, and most especially, thank you to my beautiful (inside and out), sweet, loving wife, Sherri. We are a team. Your 100 percent unconditional love makes life fun and easy. Being able to wake up each morning and go to bed each night with my best friend and soul mate is a dream come true!

Introduction

by Jay Blaushild

There are very few stories about my father, Hyman Blaushild, growing up in Riga, Latvia, because they were mostly bad stories; painful ones he didn't want to remember or tell. Back then, Jews in Latvia were persecuted regularly. They were not allowed to own land. The police could regularly barge into Jewish homes without warning or pretense, taking whatever they found in the home and arresting the inhabitants with no due process. Pogroms, campaigns of persecution or extermination directed against Jews and sanctioned by local or national governments, were common events in the 19th century. It was a backdrop to the terrifying environment in Eastern Europe that eventually erupted into World War I.

What I know about Hyman's childhood is that he entered the sheet metal trade when he was only in second grade, giving him the background to eventually establish Famous Furnace, our family business. Hyman dropped out of school to work as an apprentice for sheet metal contractors. Two of his responsibilities were to cook for the workmen and to serve them vodka—and the Russians drank a lot of vodka. When they wanted liquor, he had to be ready with a bottle.

Hyman progressed beyond cooking and serving vodka and began working in the factory with the men. With only a second-grade education, his immersion into the sheet metal industry became his education.

INTRODUCTION

When World War I began, Hyman's height saved him from the front lines. He was as short as a teenager and as an adult, only reaching about 5 feet 1 inch tall—and that proved lucky for him. In Latvia, once you reached a certain age, they would put you in the Russian army for 17 years. Because Hyman was so short, he was thought to be younger, so he was never enlisted.

When the war started in 1914, Hyman's older brother, Lester, immigrated to America. When Lester could afford to bring over another family member, he brought Hyman in 1922. Next, they brought their third brother, Bennie. Together, the brothers earned enough money to bring their mother and sister to America.

When the Blaushild family went to America, they left their memories of Latvia in the old country because most of those memories weren't worth bringing with them. Neither Hyman nor his brothers, or any of their friends from Riga, ever had any desire to go back to see where they grew up.

America was a new start—a land of opportunity for the Blaushilds. Hyman never complained about the conditions in the United States and neither did any of his friends who immigrated from Russia or Poland. No one would gripe about taxes. They saw taxes as fair compensation for the opportunity to work each day and make money without the fears and persecutions they experienced in the old country. These immigrants had a strong, enthusiastic work ethic—they had to, or they wouldn't have survived.

When Hyman came to America after WWI, he didn't speak a word of English. With his knowledge of the sheet metal trade from Europe, he picked up sheet metal work in America, mostly installing furnaces and roofs. The tradesmen he worked with here were mostly immigrants, too, so they all spoke Yiddish together. Throughout time, Hyman and his friends learned to speak English, a few words at a time, with practice. It was broken English, but you could understand them.

In the 1920s, it took an average of three days to rip out an old coal furnace and put in a new one. In Hyman's mind, that was three days the customer went without heat, and that was unacceptable. He organized his crews to start work at 6 a.m., and they wouldn't leave until the job was done. It might have been 9 p.m. or 10 p.m. by the time they finished, but they always did it in one day.

BECOMING FAMOUS

As soon as Hyman got paid for a job, he would divide up the cash, so his employees got paid immediately. He learned early that one secret to attracting people to work for you is to pay them. Hyman never missed a payroll. People left competitors to work for Hyman because they knew they'd get paid fairly and regularly.

Later on, we asked some of his first employees what Hyman did to become so successful in the early days. They answered that he did what he said he'd do, when he said he'd do it. It's so simple, but it's what would make Famous so famous. He honored his commitments.

Obviously, not everyone in the industry kept the same schedules Hyman did. He realized that wholesalers sometimes held him back from serving customers as quickly as he wanted. When he needed prompt delivery on a part, distributors might wait and ship it out after a day or two—instead of jumping in a truck to drive it directly to the customer as Hyman thought they deserved. Striving to provide the level of service he wanted, Hyman became a wholesaler in 1933 when he founded Famous Furnace.

He opened Famous because he wanted to give other contractors those things he didn't have himself, which were good service, products when you need them, fair and competitive pricing, and training. He respected the people he bought from, the customers he sold to and his associates. He treated everybody like family and wouldn't ask any of them to do anything he wouldn't, or didn't, do himself.

Hyman barely spoke English, so it was actually his brother Lester who suggested the name "Famous" for the company. Officially, the company name was Famous Furnace and Appliance Co., more commonly known at the time as Famous Furnace. The bottom of the company's notepads proclaimed, "Famous Furnace for Famous Service." It was the service, not the products, Hyman wanted to be known for. As the company eventually branched out into other products, we dropped "Furnace" and adopted the more-inclusive "Supply," and became Famous Supply. The name changed but the drive for excellent service did not.

I don't know if Hyman fully understood what a "Famous" legacy he was founding. I don't think he envisioned that, over 80 years later, his son, grandson and great-grandsons would write a book about Famous service and the Famous Family. A family that grew from the roots of the company he and his team built.

Hyman had a basic mission: to give contractors great service. He was honest, sincere, and genuine about it, which is what made him so different.

Back then, a lot of salespeople were backslappers. They'd bring customers a box of cigars and take them out drinking at night. They'd wine and dine them with food, martinis, and entertainment to make a good impression. Not Hyman. That wasn't the person he was or the way he did business.

Hyman never drank, smoked, or swore. He never even told a joke in his life. Even though his first job involved pouring vodka, he stayed away from alcohol himself. He didn't touch a drink, except for certain ceremonial circumstances, until he turned 65. That's when his doctor told him that a nightly drink would be good for his health, so he sipped a shot of whiskey every evening.

He never attended an opera or a symphony or ever went to a country club. He took me to see one baseball game and fell asleep. He enjoyed football a little more. He wasn't a big sports fan except for boxing, which was his favorite. We attended every boxing match in Cleveland, Ohio, which was a mecca for the sport.

Hyman was a straightforward, sincere man. He wouldn't boast or brag or put on airs to impress customers. In fact, he usually met with customers at the nearest corner diner; nothing fancy, but close so they could get back to work without wasting time. A man of few words, he'd simply tell them, "This is what we will do for you. We appreciate your business." His customers knew he wouldn't take them to football games or out for drinks or provide lavish entertainment, but they knew he'd be there when they were in trouble. Hyman's integrity, work ethic, and reliability set him apart in an industry of backslappers. His approach of honesty, sincerity, and fair pricing was basic, yet powerful—that's what differentiated Famous. When Hyman founded Famous in 1933, the U.S. was in the depths of the Great Depression. Far more companies were closing than were starting. About 15 million Americans were unemployed and nearly half of the country's banks had failed. Families hunkered down together to save what they could, and ours was no exception. Our family moved into my mother's parents' house, where my three aunts and uncle also lived. Eleven people, representing three generations of our family, lived together in cramped quarters during most of the Great Depression. Though times were tough, the conditions for the family were still better in America than what the family had left in Latvia. Together, we made it work. We didn't know we were poor. We knew things were tight, but the whole street was that way. Many families did not have a car; they went by public transportation. Because Hyman's brothers owned car dealerships, Hyman was one of the few people who owned a car. And, because he was in the sheet metal business, the family never went without a furnace or water heater. Famous had a fairly solid footing during the Depression because people still needed warm homes, hot water and roofs over their heads—even if they couldn't afford much else.

This fragile economic environment taught Hyman to be modest in business. He started with a delivery fleet of just one truck. He bought buildings rather cheap—which meant they weren't necessarily beautiful, but they were affordable. Like the contractors he served, Hyman didn't care about the outside of the building as much as he cared about the products, prices, service, and, most importantly, the people inside.

Hyman invested in the essentials—people and products—that would make the company "Famous" for service. He kept those priorities straight, despite the economic crisis. What little money the company made went right back into it, so he could make improvements. In 1939, Famous made $400 and allocated half of it to installing a new floor in the office. Hyman never took a dividend. To this day, the Blaushild family invests 100 percent of the profits back into the company and to our associates.

Hyman didn't see the Depression as a detriment to launching or growing his wholesale business. For him, success came down to working harder—in good times or bad. He had a dream and a vision that if you worked hard enough and put what little you made back into the company, you'd have a little more inventory or people to serve customers better. Then, every day gets better than the day before.

From a young age, I watched my father's passion for the business and began to love working. By age 5, my favorite hobby was collecting deposit bottles to turn in for refunds. With my hard-earned bottle money, I bought my first hamburger. I can still tell you the restaurant I bought it from, how much I paid for it, and which booth I sat in to eat it.

My friends and I shoveled driveways, mowed lawns, and offered others in the neighborhood various services to make money. I was always working—some jobs I enjoyed, like selling shoes or burning garbage at a supermarket. Others, like setting pins at a bowling alley, I didn't like so much. I saved money to buy myself a baseball glove (the only one I ever owned). In third grade, I bought a bicycle that lasted through high school.

Like many kids who grew up during the Depression, I had a saving mentality paired with an enthusiasm for work that my entrepreneurial father instilled. We took pride in earning money. We didn't like taking money from our parents because we saw them work so hard to get it. We wanted to make our own.

When I was 5 years old, my mother fell ill, and Hyman sent me to a military summer camp for children. I was the youngest camper there. I loved baseball, shooting, horseback riding, boxing, canoeing, tennis, and camping as much as anyone there. The campers wore uniforms and marched everywhere they went. It was tough—but the discipline was part of what I enjoyed about it.

We got an inspection every morning and if one person's bed wasn't right, they would punish all of us. There would be no horseback riding or canoeing that day. So, we learned to take care of each other; we had each other's backs. We loved the discipline, and it taught us teamwork.

I learned self-discipline at a young age. My mother passed away when I was in second grade, and soon after that, my brother, Donald, got sick and died. My father later remarried, but I had learned to take care of myself. As young as 7 or 8 years old, my buddies and I would camp out in the woods for a few days or take canoe trips together on Lake Erie.

Today, parents get nervous if kids cross the street without a cell phone, but it was a much different world then. I would never send a third-grader alone to walk through downtown Cleveland today, but back then, I would leave my elementary school and make my way across Cleveland's East Side to get to the Famous branch.

I'd take a streetcar and several buses from East 36th Street and Euclid to East 55th Street, and then hop on another streetcar to Woodland Avenue, where I'd walk to East 64th Street, arriving at my father's office. I'd entertain myself there until my father drove us home at the end of the day. I literally grew up in the family business.

By the time I was about 13 years old, I started working in the warehouse. I swept floors, stocked shelves, cleaned trucks, and emptied garbage. A manager once assigned me bathroom cleaning duty, making me wash and scrub the toilets for inspection. I hated it, but I had done such a good job the manager kept assigning it to me. There were no breaks for the boss's son.

I didn't realize then that even the dirty jobs were preparing me to lead the company one day; maybe I knew all along. I learned that you do what has to be done. I just loved working hard. It's hard to believe, but I knew as a little boy I would go into the family business.

All along, Hyman was instilling the traits and values in me that would prepare me to take over the company. The lessons didn't necessarily have anything to do with business; they were more about common sense.

Even as Hyman picked up the English language, he never learned to write it. Until the day he died, he could only write his name. But, somehow, he taught himself to read, and he'd get three newspapers every day. He read every page of every paper, including the classifieds. Then, he'd pass me the papers and quiz me about the day's events.

He had the best memory of any person I ever knew. Growing up, I thought I had a very poor memory because I was comparing mine to his—until I found out later in life that I had a fantastic memory. Hyman continued to sharpen my memory, the same way I later quizzed my son, Marc, and he did the same to his sons, Brian and Kevin. When I was a teenager, for example, my dad would question me about inventory in the stores they visited.

After we'd visit branches, we'd get in the car and my father asked me, "How many 40-gallon heaters were there?"

"I don't know," I replied. "Well, you were there. Didn't you count them?" "No, dad." So, the next visit, I'd count in my head. My father asked again, "How many

40-gallon heaters were there?" "Twenty." I was ready this time. "There were really 19, but that's good; you're close." He taught me to look, hear, and remember what I was observing. They say 90 percent of what we hear we forget within 24 hours. My father didn't believe that. He said, "Whatever you hear, you should remember forever."

My father's office on Woodland Avenue housed about 4,000 miniature liquor bottles on shelves around his office, comprising one of the largest collections of its kind in the United States. The most impressive thing about the collection was he remembered every detail about each one. Amazingly, he remembered where he purchased every single bottle and how much he paid for it. We recently moved a portion of the bottles to our new headquarters where it's prominently displayed as a reminder of our humble beginnings.

Hyman's excellent memory extended into the business, too. He remembered all the products he sold, to whom he sold them, who owed him money, and what the cost figures were from last year or even two years ago. He memorized every aspect of the business. He remembered the names of everyone who worked with him, their interests and hobbies, and the names of their spouses, children, and pets.

His memory helped him build and maintain meaningful relationships. He knew about and understood people, so he could serve them better. Because he knew his inventory so intimately, he could connect people with the products they needed to add value.

That's why memory is crucial to business. Even though a lot has changed since Hyman founded Famous over 80 years ago, many of the principles Hyman built into the business are timeless and critical to our success and survival. It's important for us to keep remembering and retelling the stories that have been foundational to our success—and the missteps that have taught us valuable lessons.

By remembering history, you remember both the good and the bad, and those things guide you in future decisions. History is a foundation we build on, and the more we remember that, the better our future will be.

EARLY GROWTH

Chapter 1

Building Our Famous Culture
as told by Jay Blaushild

If you ask anyone about the foundational key to Hyman Blaushild's success, you'll hear about his keen ability to hire great people. Today, we use Jim Collins' terminology from the book Good to Great to say he put the right people in the right seats on the bus—but Hyman did it long before it was a book. My father had an unbelievable ability to pick out winners—people who had character, work ethic, intelligence, pride, and who wanted to create something great. Not only did we energize the initial associates, they energized us. Everyone worked together to develop the culture we created. Hyman didn't see color or gender in candidates—which is noteworthy considering the racial equality gaps that existed. He didn't care if the interviewee graduated from college or high school, since he himself had only finished second grade.

He asked question after question to learn about the character of each candidate, digging to uncover qualities like enthusiasm, honesty, and curiosity. My father believed in complete interviews—we spent as much time with as many people from our company as it took, and I would listen in on many of them. You couldn't do this today, but one question he always asked near the end of the conversation was, "Do you go to church on Sunday?" He never asked what church; he didn't care. He thought if a person had faith, they would be a better person for the company.

He asked candidates about their school interests, extracurricular activities, family upbringing, and previous jobs. Today, there are laws for what we're legally allowed to ask in interviews, but the interviews still embrace Hyman's underlying goal; to reveal who the candidate is as a person, and their skill-set.

Competitors' associates frequently came to Hyman saying they wanted to work at Famous. He'd ask them why. If they replied in numbers, explaining how they'd make more money at Famous than at their existing job, he'd politely tell them to stay in their current position. Unless you have an in-depth discussion, you can't uncover what the person's attitude, desires, and visions are. If those things aren't in alignment with Famous' culture, it's better for both parties if they're never hired.

My father was serious about hiring associates who shared his values, and equally serious about removing the ones who didn't. He wanted to see each candidate through as many sets of eyes as possible. He'd have several other associates conduct their own interviews. Eight or nine interviews might take place to hire a forklift driver. These conversations often happened in casual settings during breakfast, lunch, or in the cab of a truck if we were hiring a driver. By involving his team, the whole company got to know each candidate better.

After the interview process, Hyman insisted potential candidates bring their spouses into the office, so they could assess the opportunity together. He wanted wives to see where their husbands would work and to understand the demands of the job, even if it meant a few late nights. Hyman was a family man, and he wanted hires to know they were joining a company that cared about their families.

If any stage of the interview process revealed red flags, Hyman didn't hesitate to tell candidates they weren't the right fit. He knew a square peg would never fit in a round hole, and everyone would be better off parting ways.

The interview process allowed us to hire those who fit and, more importantly, to not hire those who weren't the right fit. This diligence helped create the company we have today.

As Famous grew to six people, then to eight, 12 and 14, Hyman thought of his team as a family. After selecting them so carefully in his thorough interview process, he wanted to make sure they felt valued. Every year around Christmastime he threw a celebration called the Famous Annual Banquet. Associates who came brought their families along for a festive dinner that felt more like a family Thanksgiving than a formal corporate event. Now, with more than 1,000 associates in Famous Enterprises, it's more difficult to get everyone together, but the feeling we have for our associates doesn't waiver.

Hyman gave $100 to each associate who got married or had a baby during the year, which was a very generous gift back in the 1930s and 1940s. He even let newlywed associates borrow the company truck to go on their honeymoons to Niagara Falls because most people didn't have their own cars. Those little acts of appreciation solidified the Famous Family as the company grew.

Hyman didn't do a lot of talking, but he made a point of communicating with his team. Most of what he said came in the form of questions. When the phones stopped ringing at the end of the day he'd make his rounds and check in with associates. He'd talk with the truck drivers, asking them what they saw, heard, did, and learned that day. Every single day before he left, he'd gather the team for an informal meeting to discuss the day's events and to make adjustments for the next day.

He asked the best questions because they made people think. Anyone could talk, whether it was a truck driver or the office manager—everyone had an equal say. We didn't have a conference room. We met in the office, out in the open, where everyone could say whatever they wanted. It was truly open, and it happened every single afternoon before everyone went home.

Ultimately, Hyman's questions boiled down to: "What happened today? What should we be doing differently? How can we improve tomorrow?" He tried to improve every aspect of every process of the business—from the products we bought, to how we stocked them, loaded them, priced them, and, most importantly in his eyes, the service with which we delivered them.

The meeting usually lasted between five and 15 minutes, but on rare occasions, it might run an hour or two if people had a lot to say. A larger meeting happened on Saturday mornings when sales associates came in from the road and the office quieted down so the team could plan for the week ahead.

Hyman's questions prompted conversation in these meetings, but it was how he responded to their answers that created an environment of open, honest communication.

He never disciplined someone for saying something he didn't agree with. That created an environment where all people felt comfortable sharing their thoughts and ideas. They're the ones who know what's going on in the company and in the field, with products and with the people.

These meetings were where the first Famous associates generated many of the ideas that would shape the company. Associates often mentioned people they encountered in the field, like competitors' salespeople who were looking for new job opportunities, and that's how we have many of our associates. We've hired many associates from our own people's recommendations. We never hired from want-ads for our first 25 years.

Many of our team members have brought their friends and family members to Famous. Our people ended up working alongside their wives, sons, sisters, brothers, mothers-in-law, cousins, former colleagues, and classmates. It was a self-perpetuating cycle of growth. By referring like-minded people who shared the same values, the first Famous associates launched a snowball effect that built upon the company's founding principles. Even though we hadn't articulated our Core Values in any official documents, they played an undeniable role in establishing the company and its culture.

I once read that the first 10 or 15 people you hire determine the culture of your company. My dad never defined our Core Values or culture on paper, but he always stressed honesty, decency, and the Golden Rule. He wanted to run a good, clean company that never cheated a customer, vendor, or anybody else. People want to work for ethical companies that are honest, so living our Core Values gets us better associates. There's pride in our people when they look around and see others embracing our Core Values and our 40 Fundamentals. In that way, Hyman's first few hires built the values and the culture inside Famous. Those same people were instrumental to the company's external growth, too, as Hyman built a branch strategy tied directly to our best associates.

Chapter 2

Branching Out
as told by Jay Blaushild

In 1948, when I was 15 years old, my dad told me, "We're going to grow. We're going to open branches just like we have in Cleveland. We'll give the service, products, pricing, and training to customers out of town. We'll do what we do here; we'll just do it over there." Hyman had a vision to duplicate what he'd built on Woodland Avenue in Cleveland by expanding to more locations to create a network of stores that could readily supply contractors across the region.

When I looked at the financials, I thought: "How can we open a branch when we have so little money?" But my father didn't let our lousy financials interfere with his vision. Looking back, no one would think of opening a branch in that situation. Maybe that's why only one out of 30 or 40 wholesalers ever opened a branch; they didn't have the money or the guts.

Hyman may not have had tons of money, but he had the courage to take calculated risks for the company. He had loyal people to execute his vision. Those people were directly responsible for the company's growth as Famous expanded. If a sales associate performed exceptionally well, Hyman would let him run his own branch. The sales associates were the ones he trusted to open new locations as the company grew because they knew the markets best.

After Cleveland, the first Famous branch that opened was a 5,000-square-foot facility in Lorain, Ohio, where one of the company's strongest sales associates lived.

Next was a branch in Steubenville, Ohio, which was familiar turf for the sales associate who Hyman charged with running it. The third branch went to a top-performing sales associate in Akron, Ohio. The pattern followed as branches opened in Warren, Wheeling, and Mansfield, Ohio. Uniontown, Pa., was next. Newark and Fremont, Ohio, brought us up to 10 branches by 1962.

It was an incentive to our people that if they did a good job, we'd open a branch for them. These people had an incredible desire to run warehouses, but my dad knew great sales associates sometimes made lousy managers. He knew that unless the manager had a great inside staff to support them, they wouldn't succeed.

He didn't always know whether a sales associate could handle the role of running a branch until he gave them the opportunity. When the first manager of the Uniontown branch passed away, a sales associate from Wheeling approached Hyman and asked for the position, so he got the job. Six months later, he called Hyman back and admitted he'd made a mistake. Management wasn't so fun after all, and he wanted to go back to sales, so he went back to his old position, and Hyman hired another manager, Sonny Adeo, who ran Uniontown for 40 years until he passed away. He worked for Famous for over 50 years, like many others. It was mutual loyalty.

Throughout time, Hyman got better at recognizing and developing leadership skills in his managers. The key was giving associates opportunities to advance. Growth provided more opportunities for associates because Hyman promoted from within and encouraged people to move around inside the company. The more experience each person had performing different roles within the company, the more each one could offer. Every new branch opening required input from the entire organization. Hyman relied on everyone to pitch in.

We divided up all the products that needed to go into the new branch among all the people working in the existing branches. Each one would determine what should go in based on their knowledge of what makes a balanced inventory and they would load it on their trucks and send it to the new store. Throughout the weekend, we stocked all the shelves and were open for business by Monday morning. It was a team effort where everyone worked together to support a new branch opening.

Associates knew what they were good at and responsible for, and they all came together to tackle the pieces required to open a branch. For the Warren opening, as an example, Art Solomon, a key sales leader and branch manager in our largest markets, brought in cash registers from Akron. Former Vice President of Purchasing John Kallos brought gas furnaces and controls from Cleveland. Bill Green, a regional manager who helped lead us into new product categories, had a carpenter for a father, so he built the counters. Others painted and varnished shelves or laid flooring. Throughout one weekend, people worked 14- to 16-hour days, only breaking for church on Sunday morning, and leaving that evening after launching an entire branch together.

The process improved with every branch opening as Famous multiplied in size. When Hyman saw the growth, he realized the company was capable of much more.

My father could have stayed on Woodland Avenue and had a good, simple life. But he didn't have hobbies like horses, sports, or going on long vacations. His desire was to see what he could do. So as the company grew, his vision expanded. His vision started with new branches, then moved in new product lines to grow sales and to bring in more customers.

With a goal of 10 percent annual growth, Hyman set out to reach $10 million in sales. When he achieved that, he raised the goal to $20 million. The more success we achieved, the greater his vision became to do more. It wasn't what he could do with the money. Money was strictly a scorecard. He took incredible pride, like I do, in seeing people grow and develop. By 1955 we'd opened six branches, and I had earned an accounting degree from the University of Miami at Coral Gables in Florida. I attend law school for two years and then spent two years as an officer in the Air Force ROTC. While stationed at the Strategic Air Command Headquarters in Omaha, Nebraska, I soaked up a lot of management and people skills that later benefited the business.

I came back to Famous in 1957 with a much deeper understanding of corporate financials. When my dad talked about continuing to growth through mergers and acquisitions, my newfound knowledge of money and business led me to disagree.

I said, "Dad, I'm an accountant. It won't work. We don't have the money." He said, "We will do it. We'll get the money." Usually it's the more aggressive sons who want to take risks, but my dad had the vision and I was the conservative one. I was the one telling him we couldn't do it while he told me we'll make it work. His vision was always better than mine. He taught me that when you want to get something done, you must have the guts to do it.

We made our first acquisition in 1963: a small distributor in Sandusky, Ohio, that ushered Famous into the plumbing business. What made the move even bolder was that we were opening a new branch about 20 miles away in Fremont, Ohio, at the same time. Before we completed the acquisition, a Canton, Ohio competitor called my dad offering to sell his company. Again, I was cautious about the financials, but my dad charged ahead.

It always worked out. It wasn't magic, guts, or luck that grew Famous. Hyman wasn't taking stupid chances or blatantly ignoring what the financials showed. He put a lot of thought into each decision, so it was less about luck and more about the acronym L.U.C.K.—Laboring Under Correct Knowledge. Hyman had an incredible understanding of the business and he had an amazing memory for every detail down to the dollar.

My dad had guts and intuition, coupled with the knowledge of how the money would flow. He had a mind for cash flow. Every day, for every warehouse, he knew their credit sales, their collections, and their cash sales. When we needed cash to pay our bills by the 10th of the next month, he knew in his mind how we would have it.

Early growth wasn't always smooth and easy. There were tough situations, and there were a few times when Hyman's brothers floated Famous a quick loan until receivables came in.

Some companies aim to break even after two or three years, but Hyman was determined to make each branch profitable within the first month of opening. It wasn't always much, but new branches stayed in the black from the start. Famous never missed a payment to a vendor, a paycheck to an associate or any other financial commitment because Hyman always had enough money coming in to pay every obligation. To this day, we've continued that pattern.

With two acquisitions completed, Famous opened its 13th branch, in Ashtabula, Ohio. Hyman saw the company achieve his goal of $20 million in sales just before he passed away in 1970. He'd been in perfect health until the last year of his life, which he spent in and out of the hospital. At that point, he asked me to sit at his desk as acting President. I officially took the title after my father's passing and led Famous into the second generation.

My whole life had been a transition into this role. Maybe not as a little boy sweeping the warehouse, but I knew I'd eventually be President one day. I entered the role humble and scared. The day my father died I gave away my snow skis because I was afraid of breaking a leg. It scared me to think about what would happen if I wasn't there.

The transition was seamless, though, because of the incredible support I got from 98 percent of my people. There were two people who didn't think I should be President and kind of bucked me; "He's in his 30s and he's not capable to run it," they thought. I had to let one person go, and the other turned around 180 degrees and became one of the most supportive people I had.

A few weeks after my dad died, I called all 13 branch managers to a meeting where I announced significant changes to the organizational structure.

I recognized that I couldn't have everyone that reported to my father continue reporting directly to me. It was too much, so I set up three regional divisions. The branches would report to the Regional Managers, and the three Regional Managers would report to me. I still kept in complete contact with the others, but it relieved a strain off my back.

I shared my father's motivation for growing Famous, which was to continually provide better service. As I settled into the leadership role, I became more like my father in many ways. Before, I was the conservative son reluctant to take chances on his father's ambitious growth initiatives. Now, I began aggressively growing the business. Suddenly, I was announcing plans to buy a troubled sheet metal manufacturer. Others played the cautious role, asking how an acquisition could work when it was losing money every month.

But my instincts were as correct as my father's. We bought the underwater furnace pipe, duct and fittings sheet metal company, with $1.3 million in debt, for $1 and turned it into a successful part of the Famous umbrella in 1982, changing its name from LB Manufacturing to Heating & Cooling Products. Like my father, I had the instincts and insight to know these risky moves could, and would, end well. We made 13 acquisitions during my tenure as President. All, with one exception, made money in the first month.

Chapter 3

Empowered to Grow

as told by Jay Blaushild

In the beginning, we opened branches and gave incredible autonomy to the local manager. Sometimes when I visited a branch, the manager introduced me to customers as his boss and they would remark, "Oh, Art, I thought you owned the company!" I loved it. That was my favorite feeling. People thought our managers actually owned their branches, which showed that we truly empowered them.

Early on there were no computers, no fax machines and no copy machines, so we had to empower people to make decisions. We couldn't micromanage even if we wanted to because we weren't inside every branch. The only way to communicate was by telephone or in person.

We periodically got together for group buying and setting up sales and marketing programs. I put the arrows in the Branch Manager's bows, and they would release them. A lot of the other decisions were up to them. If they wanted to open the branch at 6 a.m. instead of 7 a.m., they could.

Each branch did its own pricing. I would type out price sheets, but they were a suggestion, not a decree. The people knew their markets and could set special pricing, collect their own money and set their own credit limits with customers.

Each branch determined how much of each product they wanted to put on the shelf. One place might have wanted 15 boilers; while another manager may have said, "I don't want boilers. If I sell a boiler, I'll pull it from another branch." We let the people, who knew their customers and their competitors best, make their own inventory decisions. We empowered our purchasing people to buy whatever they wanted.

At one point, I was the company's Credit Manager, Sales Manager, Purchasing Manager, Operations Manager, Accounting Manager, etc., all in one. But as the company grew, we had the privilege of hiring great associates to own these functions. It became easier for me to lead the company and for each manager to run his or her branch.

When you have specialists focusing on their particular areas of expertise, it allows the company to thrive and grow. It was far easier to have specialists run operations, purchasing, sales, etc., than to have my managers or I worry about all of it. We had Product Managers to focus on hydronics, air conditioning and other categories. Because people could focus on their primary responsibility without worrying about other details, everyone became more successful.

But back then, we were just a little plumbing and heating distributor with roofing supplies and a few other products, and our managers were entirely responsible for everything at their branches. We broke into some new product categories through acquisition, but a lot of our product expansion came from the branch managers who built their own relationships with suppliers to stock what their local customers needed locally.

One person said, "Out in the country where we are, people have wells and they need pumps for their wells. I know of a company we can buy pumps from. Can I bring in pumps?" So, we started selling pumps. Another said, "We've got customers here that need kitchen cabinets. There's a guy up the river that builds them. Can I bring in kitchen cabinets?" So, we began offering our customers kitchen cabinets. Someone else suggested, "Let's get into replacement windows." We got into replacement windows, too.

We listened to our people's ideas for kitchens, siding, countertops, and other products. For quite a few years, many of our branches sold a lot of paint because there was a company that manufactured paint a few blocks away from the Wheeling branch.

We listened as our associates told us what they thought would work. Did everything work? No. Did we do everything they suggested? No. But we listened to their ideas and implemented many of them into the company.

The diversity of products we offered kept changing because the products we sold and the ways we sold them came from the people with whom we worked. My father knew nothing about plumbing before we acquired a plumbing company. I knew nothing of kitchens, other than eating in them, before we offered kitchen products. With our people leading the way, we grew beyond HVAC and into plumbing, building products, and industrial pipes, valves, and fittings.

There was a lot of trial and error. When we got into pumps, one manager wanted a vendor he preferred, and another manager wanted a different brand. So, we let both buy the pumps they wanted then watched to see which one worked best. We did that a lot because the managers knew their customers and their local areas. They had better relationships with some manufacturers than I did at corporate. We never punished anyone for making an error by picking the wrong product; we learned from our mistakes as much as our accomplishments.

That means our managers also had authority to stop stocking common items that weren't selling for them. One of our core products used to be a brand of asphalt roofing. A manager in Warren, Ohio, said, "It's taking up too much space. If we could get rid of it, I think I could put the money and space into this other product instead." We told him, if he wanted to get rid of it, get rid of it.

Thanks to our people's ideas and suggestions, we brought on new products that sold well and got rid of ones that didn't. One pitfall in business is getting emotionally attached to product lines and the people who sell the products. If sales are going down and not coming back, it takes courage to get rid of products that aren't working in the same way it takes courage to get rid of an associate who isn't working.

The people who work at Famous have always been more important than the inventory, the geographic location, the size of the building, or the size of the fleet. It's all about people. It's people who made the company and grew it from one office to a distribution network of branches. Our people had the ideas to introduce the new product categories that make up our core today. It's all about people and they've always been Famous' No.1 asset.

FAMILY

Chapter 4

Family First

as told by Marc Blaushild

My grandfather, Hyman, understood his customers and the basics of the wholesale business—getting the right products to the right place at the right time, and selling them at a fair and competitive price. My father, Jay, understood it too, and grew the inventory and the business from the foundation Hyman built.

They also understood something more important: opening more branches and selling more products wouldn't sustain success for the long term because the wholesale business is more than sales and transactions. Business is all about relationships, and each transaction results from healthy relationships between customers, associates, and vendors. Contractors can go anywhere to buy the supplies they need, but the difference comes from the people who sell them products, and the way they provide service. That relationship can mean more to customers than the price of the product.

Our team is determined to continuously improve how Famous associates work together to provide service to, and build relationships with, our customers. In 2016, we introduced our "40 Fundamentals for Living the Famous Way." It's the way we strive to do business with our associates, customers, suppliers, and partners, who we call "The Famous Family."

Our purpose at Famous is "To Build Meaningful Relationships for Life."

We want to be more than an employer, customer, or a supplier; we want to be friends, confidants, and trusted business partners. We're as loyal to our associates, customers, and suppliers as they are to us. We want these stakeholders to know they can count on us in the way they would depend on their own families.

From the beginning, my grandfather was intentional about building this family philosophy at Famous. His acts of appreciation, like the annual banquet or the gifts he gave to new families, solidified the Famous Family as the company grew.

The southern district's annual banquet is probably my earliest memory of Famous. I specifically remember traveling to Wheeling, West Virginia, for the company party at Oglebay Park when I was 5 years old in 1968. I can't tell you what we ate or what we did that made the party so memorable. What I do remember about the celebration is the people who were there, and I can name some of them today because many are still with the company or recently retired.

As I grew up, I spent more time at Famous and got to know our associates. My parents divorced when I was 5 years old, so I moved around Cleveland frequently as a child, often hopping from one school to the next. During my elementary years, I remember going into work with my father at the Woodland Avenue branch in Cleveland—the same one he used to walk to after school to meet his father. I was only 7 years old when my grandfather Hyman passed away, so most of the stories I heard about him came from people who had worked with him. Many of them considered Hyman as much a part of their family as I did. I would also learn that many associates looked to my dad as a father figure of their own.

Growing up in a family-oriented business, my definition of family extended beyond biological relatives. Through separation, divorce and remarriage, step-parents and step-siblings became part of my extended family. Meanwhile, at Famous, I grew to become as close to some associates as my immediate family. Instead of just having a father to teach me valuable life lessons, I had an extended family of people modeling the values my grandfather had lived. Though I was born into a Famous Family much larger than the Blaushild bloodline, that didn't mean I was born into the family business. My last name didn't determine whether I would join the company; it was determined by a serendipitous phone call one summer night.

Chapter 5

The Call that Changed Everything

as told by Marc Blaushild

I didn't grow up assuming I would join the family business one day, but looking back, there were indications that the distribution business already had a hold on me as a young child.

By the time I was in third grade, I was using the distribution model to run my own operation at school. I saved money from trading baseball cards, and took my savings to Miller Drug, a corner drugstore on the east side of Cleveland near my home. The store typically sold Now & Later taffy in small packs of 10 candies, but I asked to buy a whole case. They looked at me funny but agreed to sell me full boxes for a few dollars.

I took my bulk candy purchase to school and resold it by the piece. I figured out my cost was a nickel per piece, and I sold them for a dime each, which was a 50 percent gross margin. I realized I could make money by buying bulk and selling individual pieces. Everywhere you turned at school, kids were chewing Now & Laters. It became a disruption, or so the school's authorities thought, and they shut down my little business after a few months.

When I was in fifth grade, my mother told me she, my step-dad, my younger brother, and I were moving to California. We packed up and moved across the country, and I spent the next seven years on the West Coast in the valley of Los Angeles.

I attended a large junior high school in California with over 2,000 students. The school was so big it had its own store that sold snacks and school supplies throughout the day. We had a 22-minute break in the morning, from 9:58 a.m. until 10:20 a.m., and students would wait in line to buy food and supplies, hoping they would make it to the front before the bell rang.

I noticed there were long lines every day, and they moved slowly. I saw that the school wasn't meeting the demand for snacks and supplies efficiently. So, just like I'd done with Now & Later candy in Cleveland, I bought bulk supplies of the most popular items kids were waiting for: pencils, papers, pens, etc., and kept a stock of these supplies in my bag. I tried to rush through the line to get my food at the beginning of our break, and then I sat by the back of the line to sell my goods. "Hey, what are you looking for?" I asked students waiting in line.

"I need a few pencils," someone might say. So, I sold them a few pencils.

I was running a wholesale distribution operation that met a need faster and better than the other options students had to buy supplies. I was proud of myself for helping my fellow students. That was until a school administrator approached me for a little talk. After about a month in business, my latest distribution ring got shut down again.

Every summer when school let out I came back to Cleveland to spend my breaks working in the Famous warehouse sweeping and cleaning like my father had done in his early teen years. One of the toughest jobs I did was going to the city dump each week with one of our warehouse associates, Homer, to save the company some money, and I can still remember the smell! My father had done the math and insisted it was more cost-effective to fill up 55-gallon drums with trash and haul them to the city dump every Saturday than it was to rent a dumpster and have our trash picked up. That work helped me appreciate what our warehouse and truck drivers do for Famous. Although I grew up in and around the family business, I didn't consider it my future career, much less my family legacy. For me, it was just a summer job.

At the end of my last summer as a high school student, I couldn't wait to get back to California and start my senior year. I was looking forward to two-a-day football practices, girls, playing baseball, driving my car, and seeing my friends again. Excitement was brewing as my brother and I packed our bags for our flight back to California the next morning.

Then the phone rang. My dad answered it and as he handed me the phone said, "I think you should take this." I held it to my ear and heard my mom's voice on the other end. She explained that she and my stepfather were getting a divorce. "Now is not a good time," she told me, "so I don't think you should come back to California. You should probably stay in Cleveland to finish your senior year."

That phone call marked a defining moment that changed my life. If the phone had never rung that day, I would have boarded that plane and probably followed a different path. That phone call kept me in Ohio, where I went to college, met my incredible wife, Sherri, raised our family, and started my career at Famous.

Looking back, I'm surprised I didn't just fly out to LA anyway and rent an apartment, so I could graduate with my friends as planned. Usually, if I have my mind set on something, I'm determined to make it happen. For some unknown reason, I hung up the phone and felt peace and contentment about the unexpected change. My brother and I took our luggage back upstairs, unpacked, and enrolled in our new school.

I spent my senior year at Beachwood High School on the east side of Cleveland. If I would have graduated in California, I would have gone to college out west, either at UCLA or the University of Arizona. Because I graduated high school in Ohio, I went to The Ohio State University. I didn't even apply to any out-of-state colleges. At OSU, I started dating a beautiful (inside and out) girl. I knew Sherri in high school, but we didn't date until college. Maybe fate had taken me to OSU to reconnect with her. We were engaged the week before graduation and then married within a year.

After graduating in 1985, my dad called me to discuss a position at one of the company's divisions, Famous Telephone. If I had ended up in California, I doubt I would have joined the family business at all.

When I was younger, I always said when I grew up, I wanted to either be a football coach or manage investment funds. It's ironic that, indirectly, I'm playing both roles at Famous nearly 30 years later. Every day I'm part of a team, coaching players and managing assets. I guess that's living my dream. In that sense, being at Famous is all I ever wanted, or was meant to do.

Chapter 6

Joining the Famous Family

as told by Marc Blaushild

Although I was born into the Famous Family, I remember the exact moment I realized I was part of a larger bond that extended beyond my immediate family.

On April 10, 1990, our son, Brian, was about 21 months old, and Sherri was pregnant with our second child, Kevin. While we were at a holiday dinner, a large industrial pot of coffee accidentally fell on Brian, and he was severely burned. He was in the hospital for a long time, went through a major surgery for second- and third-degree burns and underwent intensive therapies to correct the damage. It was so serious that his doctors weren't sure if he would survive the accident. Sherri was so ill from the stress of the situation she could have lost Kevin as well.

Family was my only priority, and my Famous colleagues understood. I used a hospital pay phone to call into work periodically, and my coworkers assured me everything was under control and to just focus on my family.

Those check-ins didn't prepare me for what I found when I finally got back to the office after nearly a month at the hospital with Brian. Not only was there a nice card waiting for me, but my desk was clean—cleaner and more organized than it had been before I left. My coworkers had done all of my work, and they did it as well as I could have done it myself.

That was the moment when it truly resonated within me: Famous is a family and we support each other the way a family should. Everybody pitched in to take care of me during the toughest time in our lives, and Sherri felt their support as much as I did; everyone had my back. Brian made a miraculous recovery, and Sherri later gave birth to another healthy boy, Kevin. Our immediate family was whole and happy. I will always remember the support we received from our Famous Family.

The culture of caring is woven into the fabric of Famous. It ran through the veins of Hyman and the first people he hired. Those values have endured the test of time by attracting more of the same type of people. Associates across the company have stories just like mine, many recalling a specific moment when they first knew they were part of the Famous Family.

"Sometimes it takes someone several years after they're hired to appreciate that," my father says. "Sometimes, people appreciate it the first week because they can tell a difference from experiences they had at other companies. My dad used to say, 'The longer they're with us, the more they appreciate that we are a family.'"

For Tanja Kozul, who joined Famous in 2003, that moment came after she delivered her first child at the Cleveland Clinic. She had been working with us for only about a year and was so busy finishing up a project that day, she didn't realize she was having contractions. She drove straight from the office to the hospital and delivered her daughter, Simona, a few hours later.

In Tanja's words:

"Around midnight, the nurse came in and told me that my dad was there. I said, 'That's not possible, because my dad died 10 years ago.' She said, 'Well, there's a guy who says he's grandpa.' I told her she probably had the wrong room. Then, in comes Jay with a big bag of stuff. He even brought my husband a card to give me (in case he forgot) that said congratulations. I thought it was the sweetest thing. At that moment, I realized what it meant to work for a company that held family as a core value. I'm still amazed to this day and can't, in words, describe the amount of caring I felt."

For a lot of associates, my father is the face of that family feeling at Famous—our patriarch, you could say. Personable and charismatic, he has a knack for getting to know people and making them feel like they belong. Like his father before him, he knows how to ask thoughtful questions to establish connections with people and remembers details, so he can stay connected. He always follows up by asking whether a sick baby is feeling better, how a kid's baseball game went or how many fish you caught last weekend—that is, if he didn't already visit the sick kids, attend the games or cast a line with you himself.

"Jay would come to my children's track meets, their soccer games, their confirmations, their high school graduations," says Dave Figuly, who joined the Famous Family in 1992. "I lost my dad when I was 30 [years old], so Jay's kind of like my dad. I'd never met a guy like him. I can't end a phone call with one of my kids before they ask, 'How's Jay?' They grew up with him. That's just how the Famous Family works."

Dave joined us expecting Famous to be just another stop before moving on to another job. Because of the relationship he formed with my dad, and many other coworkers, his job became more fun than work, and his colleagues felt more like family. So, he stayed.

"Somehow, four years became six, six became 10, then 10 became 20, and I'm still here," says Dave, who started as Corporate Credit Manager, has managed our Central Distribution Center and performed many other roles in the company. "This has never been a job for me."

"It grows on you," says Tom Krejci, who spent over 45 years at Famous. "My father passed away at an early age when I joined Famous, and I've known Jay as a father figure all this time. I never thought of him as a boss. He was the owner, but he was truly concerned about you. When he remembers everything about you and your family, it's clear he's genuine."

That's why so many people have been with us for 20, 30, 40, and even 50 or more years. When people work here, they become part of our Famous Family, and we become as much of a part of their family as their real relatives. Sometimes, even more so. We even have associates who retire but return to work part-time because Famous is such a core part of their life.

People stay with Famous because we are family. We share the same values and goals. We trust each other, communicate openly, and work together as a team, through good times and bad, to serve our customers better each day. We take a genuine interest in each other's lives. In a business setting, it takes more effort to establish relationships, and you must be authentic. We take a true interest in people because they're a part of our family.

Building a family culture means being present in associates' lives, whether it's engaging in casual conversations or visiting them in the hospital. But to have those conversations, leaders first have to be present in the office, not isolated in an ivory tower that looms above everyone else. Any episode of Undercover Boss will show you how easy it is for a busy CEO to lose touch with front-line people. That's why for me, working my way up through the company was a critical path to leadership. It allowed me to experience the business from various perspectives. I started in the warehouse doing shipping and receiving, then moved to purchasing. I spent two years there before moving to our credit department to work in collections. I worked in marketing for several years, spent time in operations, and briefly did inside sales before I became General Manager of the Telephone Division.

Working in most of the positions in the company has helped me immensely. The more roles you can experience firsthand, the better you can interact with people in those positions because you can truly understand what the other partner needs in the equation. Our business doesn't work unless all the gears click together. Spending time in various departments helped me see the big picture of our business and how it works through the eyes of our associates.

Just as importantly, though, other associates saw me working alongside them throughout the company, which showed them I was devoting as much time, effort and sweat as they were. I believe this process is important for any leader to earn respect, especially in a family business.

It felt natural for me to work with our associates, strike up conversations with them and listen what they told me, so I could learn. Some of my most important Famous mentors were Bill Maxwell, Frank Platz, Sr., John Kallos and Tom Krejci.

When you make people and family a priority, it's easy to make time to establish a personal connection. That's what's built our company culture. "The best way I can describe the culture," says Rick Sonkin, a longtime friend, legal counsel, and business adviser of the family, "Is how Marc, Jay, Brian, and Kevin all walk the talk. In every situation that comes up, the first consideration is always, 'What is legal and what is the right thing to do?' Then, it's about making the best decision for the company and associates, every time, all the time."

1939 - 2nd Annual Famous Furnace Banquet

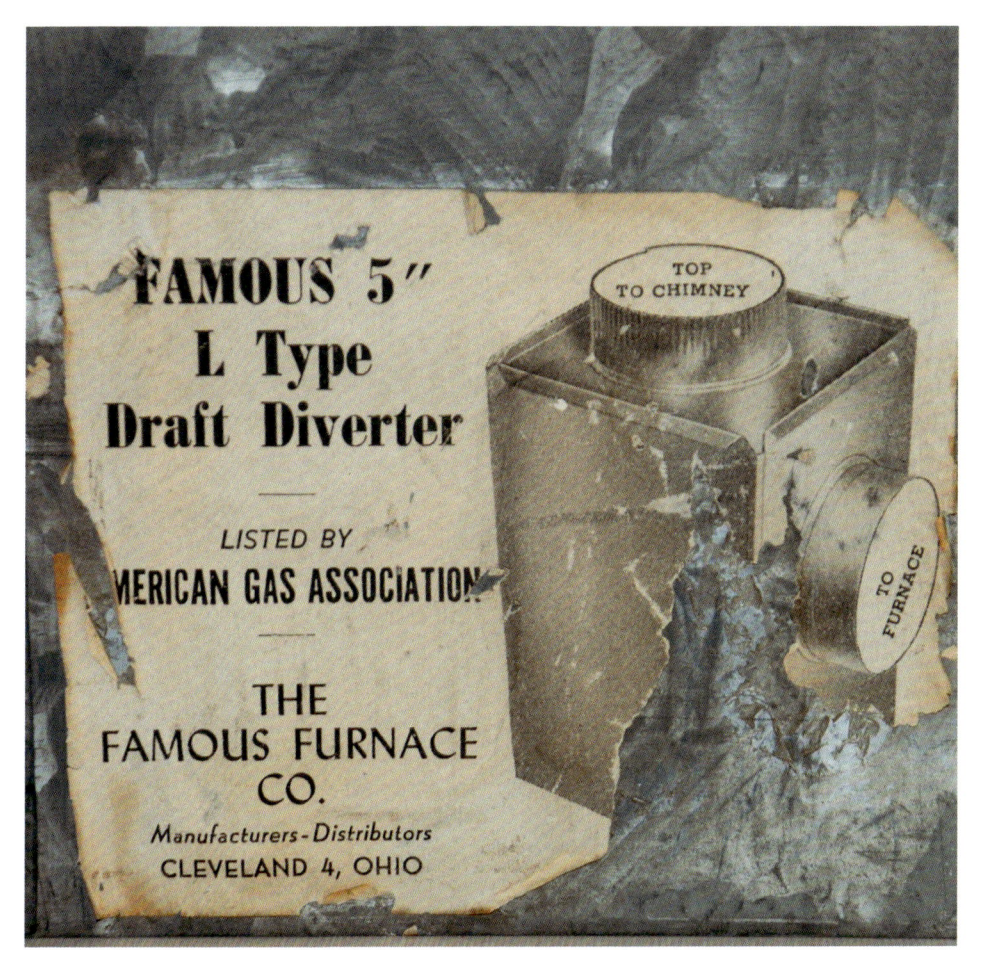

1930's - Famous Furnace Label

1946 - Hyman Blaushild, Cleveland East Office

1946 - Jay & Hyman Blaushild

1951 - Akron Branch

1951 - Warren Branch

1950's - Factory Training

1956 - Uniontown Branch Counter

1960's - Customer Pricing Look Up

1960's - Sandusky Branch

1963 - Fremont Branch

1970's - Freemont Branch

1977 - Corporate Headquarters and Distribution Center Fire

1988 - Famous Management and Leadership Training

1990 - Jay Blaushild, Tri-State Expo

2005 - Central Distribution Center (CDC) opens in Sebring, OH

2014 - Regional Distribution Center (RDC) opens in Columbus, OH

2015 - Regional Distribution Center (RDC) opens in Pittsburgh, PA

2015 - Brian Blaushild became HCP President, 2018 Jan Bauerdick became HCP President

2016 - Customer Support Center (CSC)

2016 - Brian & Kevin Blaushild

2017 - Youngstown Branch Opening

2017 - Jay Blaushild & Adam Bickford, Byesville

2019 - Famous' 1st Live Video Conference

2018 - Columbus RDC Habitat for Humanity - MidOhio Gold Partner

2019 - Canton Branch Remodel

40 Fundamentals For Living The FAMOUS Way

At Famous, our Purpose is "To build meaningful relationships for life," and we strive to fulfill that Purpose every day. Our five Core Values - Family, Trust, Communication, Teamwork, and Continuous Improvement - guide our actions and transcend generations. But what do these values look like in practice? The 40 Fundamentals that follow provide the answer. They describe the daily behaviors that define our culture and bring our Core Values to life.

1. **DO THE RIGHT THING, *ALWAYS*.** Demonstrate an unwavering commitment to doing the right thing in every action you take and in every decision you make, *especially when no one's looking*. Always tell the truth. If you make a mistake, own up to it, genuinely apologize, and make it right.

2. **EXECUTE THE PERFECT ORDER.** Provide an exceptional customer experience by striving for perfection every time, all the time. Be relentless about every detail up and down the supply chain. Demonstrate a passion for excellence. Always ask yourself, "Is this my best work?" The goal is to get things *right*, not simply just to get them *done*. Accuracy is always the priority over speed.

3. **PERSONALIZE OUR PURPOSE.** Build meaningful relationships for life by investing quality time to get to know your fellow associates, customers, and suppliers on a deeper and more personal level. Knowing more about them, their families, their work, their interests, and their aspirations is important to our long-term success.

4. **DELIVER MEMORABLE SERVICE THE FAMOUS WAY.** It's all about the customer experience. Do the little things, by focusing on the details, as well as the big things, that make someone's day. Create extraordinary experiences they'll tell others about. Do the unexpected.

5. **BE A FANATIC ABOUT RESPONSE TIME.** People expect us to respond to their questions and concerns quickly, whether it's in person, on the phone, or by e-mail. This includes simply acknowledging that we received the request and we're "on it," as well as keeping those involved continuously updated on the status of outstanding issues.

6. **SEE IT, OWN IT, SOLVE IT, DO IT.** Take personal responsibility for making things happen. Respond to every situation with a *can do* attitude, rather than explaining why it can't be done. Be resourceful and show initiative. Always stay above the line.

7. **COLLABORATE.** Work as a real team. Collaborate with each other, our customers and our partners to find the best solutions. Don't argue over *who* is right. Discuss *what* is right. Collaboration generates better ideas than individuals working alone.

8. **HONOR COMMITMENTS.** There's no better way to earn people's trust than to be true to your word. Do what you say you're going to do, when you say you're going to do it. This includes being on time for all phone calls, meetings, and promises. If a commitment can't be fulfilled, notify others immediately and agree upon a new timeframe to be honored.

9. **GET CLEAR ON EXPECTATIONS.** Create clarity and avoid misunderstandings by discussing expectations upfront. Establish mutually understood objectives and timelines for all projects, action items, and commitments. Set expectations for others and ask when you're not clear on what they expect of you.

10. **LISTEN GENEROUSLY AND WITH PATIENCE.** Listening is more than simply "not speaking." Be present and engaged. Give people your undivided attention by quieting the noise in your head, limiting distractions, and stopping the desire to multi-task. Truly appreciate other perspectives. Above all, listen to *understand*.

11. **SPEAK STRAIGHT.** Express yourself honestly in a way that moves the action forward. Be clear and direct, but thoughtful. Bring the water cooler to the meeting and have the courage to ask questions, share ideas, or raise issues that may cause conflict when it's necessary for team success. Address issues directly with those who are involved or affected.

12. **GO ABOVE AND BEYOND.** Be willing to do whatever it takes to accomplish the job . . . plus a little bit more. Take the next step to solve the problem. Go the extra mile, even if it means doing something that's not your specific role. It's that extra effort that separates the ordinary from the extraordinary.

13. **HAVE EACH OTHERS' BACKS.** No one's perfect. Look for the best in each other and provide rigorous support, including honest and direct feedback. Be willing to step into another role or help another associate when that's what's required for success.

14. **BE HUMBLE.** Don't let your own ego get in the way of doing what's best for the team. Be open to learning from others, no matter what role they have, and regardless of their age, industry, experience, or years with the company. Everyone has something he/she can teach us, and everyone's perspective has value.

15. **WALK IN OTHERS' SHOES.** Understand both your internal and external customers' world. Appreciate their challenges and frustrations. Think from their perspective. The better you understand them, the more effectively you can anticipate and meet their needs.

16. **PRACTICE BLAMELESS PROBLEM-SOLVING.** Apply your creativity and enthusiasm to developing solutions, rather than pointing fingers and dwelling on problems. Identify lessons learned and use those teachable/learnable moments to improve our processes so we don't make the same error again. Get smarter with every mistake. Learn from every experience.

17. **DELIVER RESULTS.** While we appreciate effort, we recognize, reward and celebrate *results*. Follow-up on everything and take responsibility to ensure tasks get completed. Set high goals, use measurements to track your progress, and hold yourself accountable for achieving those results. The scoreboard represents our true performance.

18. **BE POSITIVE.** You have the power to choose your attitude. Choose to be joyful, optimistic, and enthusiastic. Work from the assumption that people are good, fair, and honest, and that the intent behind their actions is positive. Give them the benefit of the doubt; and if mistakes are made, practice forgiveness. Remember that your attitude is contagious. Spread optimism and positive energy.

19. **CREATE A GREAT IMPRESSION.** Every communication, whether it's face to face, a phone call, e-mail, letter, or even a voicemail, makes an impression. Pay attention to every interaction to make sure that you're displaying a tone of friendliness, warmth, helpfulness, and authenticity. Be a pro in everything you do, including how you present yourself.

20. **BE A MENTOR.** Take responsibility, both formally and informally, to coach, guide, teach, and mentor others. The best way to influence others is through your own example. Walk the talk.

21. **COMMUNICATE TO BE UNDERSTOOD.** Know your audience. Write and speak in a way that they can understand. Be brief, accurate, and clear. Use the simplest possible explanations.

22. **"BRING IT" EVERY DAY.** Everyone is needed and everyone's important. Be present and be fully engaged. Make the most of each moment by approaching every task with energy, focus, purpose, and enthusiasm. Be all in.

23. **THINK AND ACT LIKE AN OWNER.** We share in our success. Make decisions by reminding yourself, "This is *my* company and *my own* money." Think globally about Famous Enterprises, not just about you, your department, your branch, district, or group. Ask yourself, "Will this help all of us succeed?"

24. **EMBRACE CHANGE.** What got us here is not always the same as what will take us to the next level. Be inspired by the opportunities that change brings, rather than stubbornly holding on to the old ways of doing things. Be flexible and open to new approaches, whether it's technology or a new process to improve efficiency.

25. **BE RELENTLESS ABOUT CONTINUOUS IMPROVEMENT.** Regularly reevaluate every aspect of your role to find ways to improve. Don't be satisfied with the status quo. "Because we've always done it that way" is not a valid response. Find new and innovative ways to get things done better, faster, and more efficiently.

26. **WORK WITH A SENSE OF URGENCY.** Work as quickly and productively as possible, but never sacrifice quality or safety. Don't put off till tomorrow what can be completed today. Deal with it now. Act decisively. Hustle. Get stuff done.

27. **SHARE THE WHY.** Before others can understand *what* to do or *how* to do it, they must first understand *why*. Explain the big picture. The more people understand the reason for what we're doing, the more actively they can participate in the solution.

28. **THINK SAFE. WORK SAFE.** Know and practice the safety procedures for your job. Watch out for the safety of your teammates as well, for we're all part of the Famous Family. *Never* take shortcuts that compromise your safety or that of your teammates.

29. **BE AN EXPERT.** Our customers expect us to not only offer quality products, services, and solutions, but also to be technical experts. Take the time to learn everything you can. Ask questions and do research to make yourself an expert. Be a lifelong learner and take ownership for your personal development.

30. **PRACTICE TRANSPARENCY.** With appropriate respect for confidentiality, share information freely. Learn to ask yourself, "Who else needs to know this?" The more people know, the better we can collaborate, and the better we can serve our customers.

31. **OBSESSIVE ABOUT ORGANIZATION.** Quality work flows from a clean and organized work place. Make sure your work area, and our facility are safe, clean, and orderly. For every minute you spend organizing and planning, an hour is earned.

32. **SHOW AN ATTITUDE OF GRATITUDE.** Recognizing people doing things right is more effective than pointing out when they do things wrong. Focus on people's strengths and regularly extend *meaningful* acknowledgement and appreciation in all directions throughout our company.

33. **ALWAYS REMEMBER THAT WE'RE A FAMILY.** Our relationships go deeper than simply being associates at work. We genuinely care for and about each other. Whether it's a kind word during a tough stretch, a friendly smile each morning, or a helping hand in stressful times, show your compassion.

34. **MAINTAIN A HEALTHY WORK/LIFE BALANCE.** Take care of yourself at home and at work. The healthier you are, the more you'll thrive personally and professionally. Balance your time between work, family life, community activities, physical fitness, and emotional/spiritual development.

35. **DON'T JUDGE. GET THE FACTS.** Don't make assumptions. There's usually more to the story than it first appears. Gather the facts before jumping to conclusions or making judgments. Be curious about what other information might give you a more complete picture.

36. **PRACTICE HUMAN CONNECTION.** Listen for, and pay attention to, the unique things that make people special. Use handwritten notes, personal cards, and timely encounters or phone calls to acknowledge them, and to show your appreciation for them. Show people you care about them as individuals, rather than as transactions.

37. **BE PROCESS-ORIENTED.** World-class organizations are built on a foundation of highly effective, repeatable systems and processes. Work to create processes for every aspect of your role, and then turn those processes into habits to achieve efficient and consistent results.

38. **TREASURE, PROTECT, AND PROMOTE OUR REPUTATION.** We're all responsible for, and benefit from, the Famous brand and reputation. Be a brand ambassador and always put your best foot forward. Consider how your actions affect our collective reputation, and act in a way that brings honor to us all.

39. **BE IN THE GRAY ZONE.** Not everything in life and work is black and white. Though we have policies and procedures, you often need to be in the gray zone, where guidelines and guiding principles are more important than following a rule. While making sure everything you do is ethical and legal, use your judgment and common sense when making decisions. If you're unsure how to handle something, talk about it with a coworker or manager and collaborate to determine the best course of action.

40. **KEEP THINGS FUN.** Remember that the world has bigger problems than the daily challenges that make up our work. Stuff happens. Keep perspective. Don't take things personally or take yourself too seriously. Laugh every day and enjoy the journey we're on together.

Famous Gives Back

- alzheimer's association
- City of Akron Police
- parkinson's Pals
- Jewish Federation of Cleveland
- S.W.A.P. Students With A Purpose
- MEDWISH REPURPOSE. SAVE LIVES.
- Hospice of the Western Reserve
- BREAKTHROUGH CITIZENS PREP INTERGENERATIONAL SCHOOLS
- North Coast Community Homes
- PlayhouseSquare
- cph cleveland play house
- CEF Child Evangelism Fellowship
- Robin's Nest Children's Home
- The Gathering Place - A Caring Community for Those Touched by Cancer
- K of C
- Make-A-Wish
- Boy Scouts of America
- Walk Now for Autism Speaks
- YWCA Greater Cleveland - eliminating racism empowering women
- St. Mary Catholic Church - St. Mary Parish Gala
- Cancer Support Community Central Ohio
- Believe in Dreams
- ALS Association
- The Friendship Circle
- bike MS - bike to create a world free of MS
- Baseball Factory
- Epilepsy Foundation Western/Central Pennsylvania
- H.E.L.P. Malawi
- VELOSANO Bike to cure.
- CBF Cleveland Baseball Federation
- Crohn's & Colitis Foundation of America Central Ohio Chapter
- Walk to Cure Diabetes JDRF
- The College of Wooster
- Preservation Alliance of Greater Akron
- Cuyahoga Community College
- ORT America
- water.org
- ranfurly homes for children
- Food Bank
- Feeding America
- Casa hogar
- Pals in Motion
- Cleveland Foodbank - The vital link between food & hunger.
- Cleveland Central Catholic High School

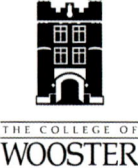

Chapter 7

Growing Up in the Family Business
as told by Marc Blaushild

As Brian and Kevin were growing up, it was important to be the best father I could be and to support them in their activities. They were both involved in multiple sports, so there were a lot of teams to support. Through a 10-year period, I coached about 50 of their baseball, basketball and football teams. Being involved in the things they loved brought me great joy, and I hope it did for them as well.

It didn't matter if I was head coach or an assistant. I relished my responsibility to be with them and had to make time for their activities. I penciled their practices, games, and tournaments into my calendar. Most days, I'd head straight from the office after work to a gymnasium or playing field. If Sherri was meeting me for a game, she might bring a sandwich; otherwise, I'd eat later in the evening when I got home. It required coordination and schedule juggling, and the boys understood if I had a business meeting or industry event that kept me from games now and then. More often than not, I could adjust my work schedule around these important personal priorities, and I love it when our associates do the same.

It was about more than just being present for them. I wanted the boys to understand balance. As important as it was for me to be present at Famous, it was even more important for me to be present at home as a father and husband. I didn't want work to seep into our family time, or to give the boys the impression that work was the only thing that mattered. I didn't want them to feel the pressure of the family business or think working at Famous was their only option.

But as they say, some things just run in the family. I brought Brian and Kevin to the office fairly often, especially when we were getting ready for the yearly trade show, because they could help stuff envelopes for mailings.

When Brian was about 5 years old, he brought one of his friends along to help. They were assisting the late Debbie Allen, who sadly passed away in early 2015. At the time, she was working in our purchasing department and preparing a mailer that was going out to customers. Brian tried to keep up with Debbie, who had years of practice on him, and he got frustrated with how fast she could stuff envelopes. As Debbie remembered:

"We were both very busy stuffing envelopes, and Brian kept comparing the amount of envelopes I had stuffed to the amount he had stuffed. I assured him that the more practice he had, the better he would be.

Brian's friend stuffed an envelope or two, then got up to get pizza. Brian looks at the different piles of envelopes, trying to keep up with me. Then, he looks at his friend's pile and notices he hasn't done very many. Brian commented that he had more, so his friend stuffed a few more envelopes before he had to take a bathroom break. He came back and stuffed another envelope, then got up to get a pop from the kitchen. He came back, sat down, put his feet up on the table and drank his pop. Brian said to his friend, 'We aren't paying you to take breaks. If you don't work, we're going to cut your pay.'"

From a young age, I knew Brian had inherited the Blaushild work ethic and desire to continuously improve.

When he told us about an assignment given to his second-grade class, I realized he already understood my work at Famous was more than just a job. He explained that his teacher, Mrs. Miller, asked his class one question: "If you could have any job in the world, what job would you pick?" She instructed them to take a minute think deeply about the question and pretend every job paid the same amount of money. Brian was torn between two ambitions. He announced to his class, "I narrowed it down to two different jobs. First, I want to be the person who collects tickets for rides at Cedar Point." The whole class laughed, and the teacher asked him to explain. "I want to ride the rides for free. But if I can't work at Cedar Point," he continued, "I'd like to do what my dad does."

When the teacher asked him what I did, he wasn't sure how to answer.

"I'm embarrassed to admit that the 7-year-old me had no idea what my dad actually did," Brian wrote in the company newsletter in 2010, 15 years after the assignment, when he decided to officially join the company. "I wish I could go back in time to that day and say to Mrs. Miller what I couldn't articulate 15 years ago: There is an expression that if you enjoy what you do for a living, then work won't feel like a job. Even as a 7-year-old, I knew that was how my dad felt about his career. I could sense the excitement and the passion for Famous that my dad possessed. While I didn't understand what inventory or receivables were, let alone what wholesale distribution was, that didn't stop my dad from sharing with me every detail about what he was doing every day."

Because of my passion for business, I'm sure I told stories at home from time to time. But it wasn't details about operations or situations at Famous. I asked my sons the questions I imagine Hyman used to ask Jay. Questions to get them thinking about business and people - how companies operate and how people interact. Brian recalls this story:

"Was there business talk at home when I was a kid? Tons—but it wasn't about Famous. We would go into a restaurant and my dad would ask me what I thought about the customer service. He'd ask, 'If you were running this restaurant, what would you do differently? What do you think they can improve?' He'd say, 'Best Buy or Circuit City: Which one is better and why?' Asking thought-provoking questions got me thinking about what companies do right, and what they do wrong. I didn't understand it back then, but he was trying to get me thinking about business. It felt like I got an MBA (Marc Blaushild Asks) before I even went to college."

I wasn't sure how much Brian and Kevin actually thought about these business questions until they started asking them. We traveled to visit my mom in California one winter break when Brian was about 7 years old, and when we arrived home, he wasn't feeling well. We took him to the doctor who diagnosed him with mono, which took him out of wrestling for the season. It upset Brian that he wasn't able to wrestle, but only for a day. The next evening, we were in his room doing a puzzle before bed when he told me about an idea he had while looking through an advertising book of mine earlier that day.

"Since I can't wrestle, I think I should start a company selling advertising," he said.

"What do you have in mind?" I asked.

"I noticed that Corky & Lenny's Deli has only blank placemats," he said, proving he was paying attention to the customer experience there. "I want to talk to Kenny (the owner) and tell him I want to give him free placemats. I can sell advertising, and on the back they can have crossword puzzles, games and coloring to make it fun for kids who eat there. How can they say no?"

I took Brian to talk with the deli owner about this opportunity with his company, which he named Brian's Biz. As he predicted, they agreed to use the free placemats.

The next Saturday, in the middle of a terrible winter snowstorm, Brian said "We're going to make sales calls today." I asked where he wanted to go, and he chose Mayfield Road because there were so many businesses there. He started with a classic: McDonald's.

When we got to McDonald's, I parked the car and opened my door to get out. "What are you doing?" Brian asked.

"I thought you said you wanted to call on McDonald's," I said.

"I do. But you wait here," said one determined 7-year-old boy. He walked inside, alone, and came back about 10 minutes later.

"How did it go?" I asked. "Not good," he replied.

"Why not?"

"They said no. They said the manager can't make those decisions, because all decisions come out of the Corporate office. We've got to go somewhere else."

"Where do you want to go next?" I asked. He looked across the street, spotted the dealership where I bought my first new car, and directed me toward it. We pulled into Marshall Ford, where we could see five big, tall, suited men talking inside. I started to get out of the car again, and again Brian asked, "What are you doing?"

"Don't you want me to go with you?" I offered. "No, no," he insisted. "I got this." I watched through the window as my little three-and-a-half-foot tall son stood in front of a group of older gentlemen, each at least six feet tall, and presented his business pitch. He came back out, and I asked how this one went.

"Not good," he said. "They said no."

"Well, what do you want to do now?" I asked.

"You know what?" he said. "Let's go down the street to John Robert's Spa. We know John and Stacy (the owners). They'll buy for sure."

So, we go there and Brian makes the sale. He comes back, excited, and proclaims, "You know what? We should call on people we already know. I don't know anyone at McDonald's or Marshall Ford. Let's go to Berger & Silver and talk to Floyd Silver."

We drove back to the other side of town, and Brian makes another sale, and then another. He even got my father-in-law to buy an ad. At a young age, Brian was already learning about the importance of relationships in the business world. He put together a well-designed placemat, sold it out a few times and donated 25 percent of his proceeds to charity.

Brian recovered from mono and went back to school and his other activities, and Brian's Biz faded into a chapter of history. But he persevered toward his idea, executed his plan and didn't get discouraged. He was a young businessman determined to succeed.

Back then, I didn't fully realize how our business discussions impacted Brian and Kevin. By sharing my passion for business, I was trying to teach them life lessons they could apply in their careers (Famous or not) and their families. Sherri and I encouraged them to follow their dreams, and it took both out of Ohio, for a while at least. Kevin recalls:

"I definitely did not grow up thinking I would work at Famous. Brian will tell you the same thing: Mom and Dad were very low pressure. They always said, 'You're welcome to work in the company. There's always a place for you, if you want it.' They told us they cared more about us being happy in life. It didn't matter if one of us, both of us or neither of us worked for the company. It wasn't as important as us being happy in whatever we did."

Brian went to Miami University of Ohio and studied accounting and finance. He got an internship in New York at Ernst & Young the summer of his junior year. He used that as an opportunity to evaluate his career options as he weighed whether he wanted to become an accountant, a consultant or work in the family business.

While in the financial sector he noticed the difference between that highly competitive environment, and the family feeling he'd experienced at Famous throughout his life. Famous gave him a glimpse of what it felt like to work with others for one greater goal, and he didn't feel that ownership at a big firm. So, after Brian graduated from Miami University in May 2010, he joined the family business.

"I knew Famous was the only place I wanted to be," he wrote in the newsletter in 2010. "I don't know who originally coined the phrase 'Famous Family,' but they truly picked the best way to describe Famous. I wake up every morning excited to come to work because I know that I'm part of something special, and every night I go to sleep proud of what we are doing here. I couldn't be prouder to work here—although free rides at Cedar Point would be nice, too."

For his first few months at the company, Brian bounced between departments to learn various aspects of the business. He spent time in marketing and credit, then traveled with salespeople to visit our locations. I wanted him to learn the operations side of the business, so he'd be prepared to manage the branch we were preparing to open in Bedford, Ohio, in 2012. He managed that facility for about a year-and-a-half.

Meanwhile, Kevin also studied business at Miami University and spent a summer internationally but wasn't sure what the next chapter would be.

Sherri recalls, "After graduation, we were sitting at a little restaurant near campus and brainstorming what his next steps were. He thought about applying to law school, but he said, 'I couldn't even get through the application; it was so boring.' He considered sports management because he loved sports. I had a friend whose brother was a sports agent, so I put them in contact. After they talked, he decided that he wanted to be in Chicago with his friends."

I reminded him that Famous had a small warehouse in Chicago that serviced our national account business, and he worked for us there. It wasn't long before he felt disconnected from the business. Around that time, the manager in the Bedford, Ohio branch was moving to a sales role, leaving us with a Branch Manager position open. I asked Kevin if he was interested in coming home and managing the branch. He agreed and stepped into the position in August 2014. With the help of the rest of the Famous Family, he got up to speed quickly and displayed tremendous leadership potential. Sherri says:

"The boys had such a wonderful foundation with a supportive father and grandfather behind them. I could instantly tell that they both shared the same passion for the business that Hyman passed down to Jay, and that Jay passed down to Marc."

You can teach your sons about plumbing and HVAC products, or wholesale distribution and dealing with customers, but you can't make them passionate about it. If parents force their children into a business they're not passionate about, the business will suffer, and the family probably will too. That's why Sherri and I encouraged our sons to find a career that made them happy. It pleased us that the opportunities for them at Famous matched their natural passions.

"Founders usually have one thing in common: a passion to do something. Many of the second, third and fourth generation (if they're there) do not have the same passion as the founders of those companies," Jay says. "But I can truthfully say, looking at my son and my two grandsons; they have the passion."

As the boys got more involved in and passionate about Famous, more business conversations came up around the dinner table at home. "It's like business is in the genes," she says. "Marc and the boys love to talk about business, and there's a lot to talk about as the business continues to grow. It's almost like a hobby of theirs, but I don't want it to take over the family time we have together. We have to work on not talking about business too much when we're home. Fortunately, they're mindful of the importance of work/life balance, so they can compartmentalize. But I have to remind them of the boundaries. It's a fine line because I don't want to squash their spirit. It's beautiful that we can share this passion for the business, and I'm very proud of them for that. But I have to make sure there's balance at home."

We try to maintain balance, but we're not as strict about the separation as my grandfather used to be. My dad told me he refused to talk business at home, period. Granted, he may have been at work until 9 p.m. or 10 p.m., but as soon as he headed home, he left business behind.

"My dad and I talked business from early morning until we got back home and opened the door," Jay says, "and then we never discussed business at home. One or two times, maybe there was a phone call. But we'd try to keep a separation and balance between business and family life."

With smartphones keeping us more connected to our work, the line has blurred, but it's still important to set aside family time at home and keep business in the office as much as possible.

SHERRI'S ROLE

We've often equated running a business to being in a family. We're built on the same principles: trust, communication and teamwork. We all depend on each other, and each of us have our roles to keep the family cohesive.

Sherri has always been one of my most trusted business advisers. Even before she understood the distribution business, Sherri could offer valuable guidance about dealing with people and treating the Famous Family right.

When I formed the Advisory Board in 2006 to provide another layer of leadership guidance, I knew Sherri's empathy and care for the company would be an asset.

"The more familiar I am with what's going on in the company, the more knowledgeable I can be when I'm speaking with our customers or our associates," Sherri says. "I may not be there 9 to 5, but I'm there at different times. Whether I'm driving to wakes, weddings, board meetings, or conference calls, I see a different side of the Famous Family."

"What I find interesting is the role that Sherri plays," says Jay Greyson, an original Advisory Board Member. "She has a full level of involvement, even though it's almost an undefined role. There is such a clear trust and love between Marc and Sherri. They look out for each other in the normal ways that couples do, but also probably in some other ways, too. She's a bright person, listens carefully and has watched all the generational changes, so she has the history. She plays a larger role in shaping the overall culture than we can measure."

Chapter 8

Famous Family Fund
as told by Marc Blaushild

Our Famous Family is the top priority for our company, and that means supporting our people, so they can put their immediate families first. We want our associates to have a work/life balance that allows them to spend quality time with their families, so we provide extra support to ensure they're able to.

We started February Famous Family Fun Night in 2006 to break up the winter blues. We encourage people to do a fun activity with their families, and we reimburse a portion of their costs. People can use the money for activities such as bowling, seeing a movie, visiting a museum, or going to a ballgame.

Every year people get excited when February approaches, so they can plan their family outings. By the end of the month, we've received tons of pictures and stories from associates sharing their memories.

"You don't understand how important that is to people," says John Palermo, a 39-year veteran of Famous and our Vice President of Sales and Branch Operations. "I don't know if any of us really understand the impact it has, but when you have conversations with associates about it, you can tell. An associate at one branch told me, 'I've never taken the kids to the movies because we're on a tight budget, and this gave me the opportunity to spend time with them.' When you hear stories like that, it's touching."

FAMOUS FAMILY FUND

We want our associates to go home and have healthy relationships with their families as much as we want them to have healthy relationships with their colleagues at work. When people are excited to come to work and not stressed about things at home, they'll be happier and will do a better job serving customers. That's the holistic approach we take to our business.

We also realize that every family has difficulties. Sometimes hardships strike, and people need help. As a Famous Family, supporting each other during tough times is even more important than celebrating together during good times. We established our "Famous Family Fund" to support Famous associates and their families when they experience tough financial situations. Many Famous associates donate a portion of their bi-weekly paycheck to the fund, raffles and fundraisers are held throughout the year, and the company provides an annual donation. The money goes to associates in need for rent, car payments and other bills..

There are two components to the Famous Family Fund, Hardship and Scholarship, and any associate can apply. If an associate needs help to pay bills, they can apply for the Hardship Fund. The Scholarship Fund aids associates or their immediate family members who are pursuing higher education by helping with the cost of books. We have a small committee of caring people who confidentially review applications to determine how to allocate the funds.

Helping fellow associates in need is the essence of our Famous Family. The associates who contribute to the fund and make efforts to raise money for fellow associates in need is proof that giving is embedded in our culture.

As of this printing, the Famous Family Fund has raised more than $140,000, granted 39 book scholarships and helped 89 associates pay a variety of bills.

Chapter 9

Being in a Family Business
as told by Marc Blaushild

When my grandfather founded Famous, most of our competitors were family-owned heating suppliers like us. As we look around the market today, most of those family businesses either closed down or sold out to large conglomerates. Even if family members maintain leadership positions after they sell, the family feel slowly disappears.

The difference at Famous is that we thoughtfully protect the Famous Family by guarding the values that shape our Famous culture. Although my grandfather didn't talk about Core Values or corporate culture, he understood how important they were to the company's success. He understood that if he took care of associates, associates would take care of customers and customers would take care of the business. I don't know if Hyman imagined how much the company would grow throughout time, but he built it to last, taking care to develop a strong foundation for the generations to follow.

My dad built upon that foundation by continuing to build a family culture where managers and associates looked to him as a father, brother or friend as much as their boss. Now, we're making sure we practice what we preach by defining our Core Values and 40 Fundamentals and instituting the Team Bonus to share the company's financial success with the entire Famous Family. Each generation may take a slightly different approach, but our priority on people and our Core Values will not waiver.

"As a family business, we want our associates to feel like they're part of the family," Kevin says. "What my great-grandfather, my grandfather and my dad have tried to build over the years is a family atmosphere where everyone works together, focused on a common goal."

Another thing that makes a family business different is that our goals are more long-term. When we're making big decisions, we think years, decades and generations ahead, not quarters.

Our family's commitment to reinvest back into the company is imperative to our future growth. It started in the 1930s when Hyman put half of the company's annual earnings into new flooring in the original office. Even minor improvements like that require a mindset that our family business is bigger than any single person or family.

Many family companies aren't looking to grow; they're looking to harvest. Some companies' next generations ask themselves, "How can we cut costs and harvest what we have?" They don't want to work 60 or 80 hours per week like their parents or grandparents did; they'd rather work 30 hours per week and play golf. They'd rather pick the apples on the tree than plant more trees and wait for the apples to grow. At Famous, we're looking to grow.

This harvest mentality has been the demise of many family businesses, especially in the distribution industry, which has consolidated rapidly over the past 20 years. Second, third and fourth generation owners realized their businesses couldn't continue operating the way they ran 10 years ago because the customers and technology are more sophisticated. Many small operations don't have the capability or the will to compete, so they either close down or sell out.

"The old saying that, 'the first generation makes the money, the second generation keeps it and the third generation blows it' is as relevant in distribution as any industry," says Jay Greyson, a former Famous board member who runs a private equity firm that invests only in distribution companies. "A company like Famous building through four generations, continuing to get stronger and competing with the largest national players is highly unusual in most fields, and extremely unusual in distribution. The work ethic transmitted to each generation, the commitment to teamwork that Marc and his sons have, and the relative humility drives that. They've done things the right way, and they will tell you they've been fortunate to work with countless associates who have adopted and lived Hyman's Core Values to move the company forward."

"The best part of being in a family business is the privilege of providing jobs and meaningful careers for many people," Brian says. "When I was growing up, my dad took a lot of pride in seeing people happy and excited to come to work, especially when so many people complain about their jobs."

We're in an amazing position where we can maintain the family values and personal relationships of a small family business, while taking on the strengths of a larger organization as we grow. But we never lose our focus. Whether it's a new product line, a new branch opening or a strategic conversation, every decision we make is for the sake of the Famous Family, not the Blaushild family.

"Marc is sensitive to the culture in the organization," Jay Greyson says. "He always talks about the Famous culture, and he stresses that constantly. Any decisions or major points that are put on the table for the Advisory Board and Executive Leadership Team always start by asking 'how does this affect the Famous culture?' The Famous Way starts with Marc and permeates through the entire organization. That is what has allowed this business to maintain its culture and keep its local feel despite its growth."

Chapter 10

Building a Legacy
as told by Marc Blaushild

I didn't really think much about the legacy of our family's business until I saw it through the eyes of a customer. At a customer appreciation event in 2014 I met a man from Mansfield, Ohio who shared with me the history of his relationship with Famous. When this man opened his business in the 1950s, my grandfather gave him the credit he needed to get started. He's been a loyal customer ever since, and his business is now in its third generation. He then went on to tell me, with tears in his eyes, how grateful he was for our long-term partnership.

When I hear stories like that from customers or suppliers who have been with us through many decades, I think about the legacy we're building. We're not in a transactional business; we're in a relationship business. We don't build relationships for this month, this quarter or this year; we build them for life.

Being a multi-generational business gives us the advantages of longevity and stability in the marketplace. It enables us to better relate to our multi-generational customers, many of whom have grown their businesses and families right alongside us.

"We have tons of customers that are multi-generational family businesses," says Dave Figuly. "Isn't it nice that we have next-generation leaders who can relate to the young leaders taking over their businesses?"

Future generations of the Famous Family aren't limited to Blaushilds. Dozens of families have been making careers at Famous for generations.

There are associates like John Palermo, whose brother, niece and brother-in-law all work in the company. Husband and wife Mark and Heidi Mapel, along with their children and several other relatives, work at Famous. Similarly, husband and wife Ed and Lora Yakubik, and their daughter Emily, have done the same.

When we find great associates like the Palermos, Mapels, Masons, Yakubiks, and Puchajdas, to name just a few, why wouldn't we want to hire another member of their family?

"Some companies have anti-nepotism rules where they won't hire relatives of somebody who works there," Kevin says. "We almost go out of the way to hire family members of our associates. When there are good people who have the values we look for, they probably raised their kids with those same values, and they'll also be a good fit in our Famous Family."

Dave Figuly, "It says a lot about the company when people urge their loved ones to come work with you. I've worked places where I wouldn't urge anybody I knew to work there. It says a lot about the organization when we have so many families who work here together."

The same thing happens externally as customers and vendors become loyal additions to the Famous Family. The relationships stretch beyond business. We become close friends with our customers, vendor reps and suppliers. They're as much a part of the Famous Family as our associates.

"If I look at some of my closest friends today, they're vendors, fellow associates and customers," Jay says. "I encourage associates to get close to our customers, so we can serve them better. They go to football games together, they take trips together, they fish together, they hunt together. Some of them go out for dinners together with their spouses. They go to each other's children's birthday parties. When you've been calling on our company for 40 years, you tend to get close."

Most wholesale distributors don't make such an effort to get to know their customers and suppliers the way we do.

For example, we know that Johnny Seder, Executive Vice President of our supplier Milwaukee Valve, loves Rice Crispy treats. We know that his wife Cheryl doubles the margarine and marshmallows in her recipe to make them extra gooey, just the way Johnny likes them. So, when he was in the hospital recovering from surgery, we sent Johnny an extra-gooey Rice Crispy treat shaped like one of the valves his company manufactures, with a valve handle bearing the company name.

"You feel that they care much more about you as a supplier, and their customers, than they do about money," Johnny says. "They've taken this relationship out of the realm of business. As a result, we do more business with them because I know they care about me so much.

"The minute you walk in, you want to hug the receptionist. The feeling of the office is not stuffy and corporate; it's fun and energizing. It's the kind of atmosphere where you feel at home. When we make a call there, we're calling on a family business and our friends, and it's much more fun calling on family businesses."

Once, Johnny dropped by our office during new associate orientation, so I put him on the spot in front of our newest Famous Family members. In just a sentence, he summarized what we want all of our associates to understand:

"The only thing I said was, 'I think your people are the luckiest people I know because when you work in a family business, people care about you as human beings... 99 percent of us don't really have that kind of career.'"

TRUST

Chapter 11

Trust is Like a Field of Horses

as told by Marc Blaushild

In life or in business, the foundation of any meaningful relationship is trust. Trust is our most foundational core value because it's a prerequisite for the others. Customers trust Famous to have their best interest at heart. They also trust us to provide the products and support they need, when they need it. We trust associates to deliver the level of service that keeps customers coming back to Famous when they have their choice of any distributor.

You could write an entire book about building trust, but we believe it's simple; be honest and do what you say you will do. Those were two of Hyman's founding principles when he started Famous.

Building trust is like filling a bucket of water one drop at a time. It takes a while to fill the bucket and it can be dumped out in an instant.

My grandfather and father laid the foundation for strong trust in our associates in the early days mainly because they had to. Before we had centralized oversight, standardized business processes or modern technology to connect the growing network of Famous branches, associates had to run their respective piece of the operation on their own. That's why Hyman was so careful about hiring the right people. He wanted to find smart, disciplined, hard workers he could trust to run their part of the business autonomously.

As my father wrote earlier, when customers met him for the first time, they didn't believe he owned the company because they always thought the manager of their branch did. Nothing made my dad happier than the undeniable tone of empowerment and ownership throughout the company. It showed how much we trusted and empowered our people, and how much they cared about our business and our customers because of it.

Many people in the company touch an order before it gets to our customer. From purchasing to receiving, writing orders, picking products, staging, loading, delivery, and billing, we trust each associate to do their job correctly along the way.

I explain trust to associates by showing a picture of horses in a big, open field, with white fences and a big barn far in the background. The barn is like our corporate office where we're giving direction and providing support. Our associates interact with our customers out in the field, and we want them to roam free and follow their instincts to serve customers.

The ultimate boundary is that whatever associates do it must always be legal, moral and ethical. We build fences around behaviors we won't tolerate, then allow our associates to use their judgment to make decisions in the gray areas.

The balance of trust and empowerment is tricky to strike. We want to scale best practices to provide consistently excellent service, but don't want to dictate standardized policies that mandate how associates should act in every situation. We couldn't, anyway, because circumstances can be unique and unpredictable.

My job as President and CEO is to provide strategic direction that keeps the company focused on the values, fundamentals, strategies, and priorities that move us toward our goals. Before we turn associates loose, it's our responsibility as a Leadership Team to find the right people, put them in the right role and give them the guidance, education and tools they need to achieve those goals.

The field is where our people connect with customers and serve their needs. That's why it's critical to empower our people on the front lines. No matter how big we get, we want to be small in the eyes of our customers so they feel like the associate they're working with can act as if they owned the company.

Our people aren't just working for the business; they're running it. We teach and trust our associates to follow the 40 Fundamentals and serve customers to the best of their ability. We trust that mistakes result from their positive intentions, and that they will hold themselves, and each other, accountable for Living the Famous Way.

As long as we are legal and compliant, we don't take a black-and-white, policy-based approach to dealing with customers. As our 39th Fundamental says, we "Live in The Gray Zone". Pete Bastulli, our CFO, says we "mix paint" and trust our people to solve customers' unique problems without approval from the corporate office.

Chapter 12

Taking Service Personally

as told by Marc Blaushild

Every day our branch locations, customers call with emergencies. Maybe a unique part on a furnace broke and they need a replacement as soon as possible to get a homeowner's heat working on a cold winter night. Before Hyman started Famous he was a contractor faced with urgent situations like these. Other distributors didn't have the sense of urgency he did, and they rarely went out of their way to help him. He started Famous to take care of the problems that others ignored. That is where the Famous Way of going above and beyond was born.

"There could be a delivery of a hot water tank that has concealed damage, and the contractor doesn't realize it until they get to the job. So, the customer calls us up and says, 'I'm in trouble. It's 10 degrees outside, there's no hot water and the tank won't fire up.' What would you do?" asks Tom Krejci, who worked at Famous from 1970 until 2018. "In my earlier days at Famous, a lot of our competition would stay closed, but we would open for emergencies. Famous is always thinking of our customer and their customer. In that situation, we would put a new water heater on a truck and drive it to our customer's job, and that's not unusual for anybody within the company."

One of my favorite stories of delivering memorable service is about the late Frank Platz Sr., our former branch manager in Lorain, Ohio. Many years ago, we had a customer who needed kitchen cabinets delivered on a Monday. We expected to receive them from our supplier the Friday prior, so we could have it at the job site on Monday. Frank found out late Friday afternoon that the supplier hadn't shipped the cabinets. They told Frank the cabinets wouldn't be on the road until Monday, meaning they would be late getting to the builder who had already scheduled an installation crew for the day. Not only was it inconvenient for the builder, but it would be expensive to reschedule their crew.

Frank climbed into one of our trucks on Sunday and drove seven hours to the supplier's Indiana plant. He slept in the cab of the truck that night and waited until the supplier opened its doors at 5 a.m. Monday. When he woke up, he loaded the cabinets onto the truck and drove all the way back to the customer's job site in Lorain, Ohio to make the delivery early Monday afternoon.

Talk about going above and beyond—Frank drove 14 hours throughout two days for a customer and didn't tell anyone about it. He did it because he wanted to solve the customer's problem, and we found out about it years later. That's one of my favorite stories because it showed someone going above and beyond without being asking, and the humility of a great man. Doing things outside of a job description for the sake of the customer, rather than the credit, happens here all the time.

Some companies might forbid employees from taking such an initiative, shortsightedly looking at the cost as outweighing the return for the business on that single delivery. But we're looking long-term at our purpose, which is to Build Meaningful Relationships for Life. From that perspective, an associate's decision to help a customer directly aligns with our purpose.

Frank, who has since passed away, was with the company for over 50 years. At his funeral, his family honored his wishes and buried him in his favorite Famous Supply shirt. His son, Frank Jr., now leads the Lorain location just like his dad did.

Another story I love takes place on Thanksgiving Day in 2001. The branch manager at our Wheeling, West Virginia location, Allan Turk, was sitting down to dinner with his new girlfriend, Patti, and her family. It was their first holiday together, and he naturally wanted everything to go well.

Then his cell phone rang, and he answered to a frantic customer. The contractor on the line needed a part for a boiler as soon as possible. Going by memory, Allan was sure his branch had it in stock. He met the customer there in 30 minutes, and explained the emergency to his understanding girlfriend, who agreed to hold the meal until he returned.

Allan got to the store, found the part the customer needed and completed the paperwork within a few minutes. The contractor explained the part was for an apartment building where 12 families lived. "Looks like they're going to have Thanksgiving at home after all," he told Allan.

Allan got back in time to enjoy Thanksgiving with Patti (who is now his wife) with a new appreciation for the work he did.

"A few minutes earlier, I was upset for having to go out on a holiday, wondering why it had to happen today of all days," Allan remembers. "Then, thinking about all the families that needed heat on Thanksgiving made me glad to work for a company that can make such a difference in people's lives. The contractor said he called four companies that day, and I was the only one that answered the phone." That self-sacrifice is the reason our customers trust us to take care of them.

Another one of my favorite stories is about Carl Green, an associate who has been with Famous for over 50 years. One winter evening in 1998 we had a training program for customers and associates in Wheeling, West Virginia. The training session ended at 9 p.m., and Carl and I walked out to the parking lot together. Despite the time and frigid weather, he didn't seem to be in a hurry.

"You got a minute?" Carl asked. I said "sure," thinking he wanted to talk about something important.

"Follow me," he said, and he got in his car. I got in mine and followed him about five minutes to a job site with one building fully constructed and another in progress. He jumped out of his car excited to tell me all about the products Famous supplied for the first building.

It was dark and cold, but he kept going. He pointed to the second building and explained all the materials we were supplying for that one, telling me about the reps and suppliers he worked with to make it happen. He went on and on about the project.

"Carl, aren't you cold?" I finally asked, shivering in what felt like a zero-degree wind chill. I knew he'd been up working since 5 a.m., as always. His pride and passion for the project he worked on fueled him. He wasn't worried about the clock, the temperature, the drive home, or that he had to get up early for work the next morning. I could feel his excitement for our business, and that energized me on that dark, cold night. The passion that Frank, Allen, Carl, and so many others breathe is the essence of Famous.

One of the best things about our business is that associates feel the benefit of treating customers well, and not just financially. Everything we sell serves a function, so we're not just providing products. We're providing comfort, whether it's heat, running water, cool air, accommodations for a disability, or creating someone's dream kitchen. It's a wonderful feeling to help others. That's why our associates take service so personally and go above and beyond.

"It's not that you're just doing it for them," Jay says. "You end up doing it for yourself because as you drive back, you get that great feeling you did something wonderful to solve a problem for another person. Many people think customers buy on price alone, and the only important thing is getting something for the cheapest price. It's not true. Our customers value when someone helps them. Whether you help them change a flat tire, provide an extra service or give them an honest answer. Even if you don't make a dollar, you helped solve a problem. They trust us because you help them."

Stories like these are proof that associates are embodying our purpose and taking extreme pride in the work they do as part of the Famous Family. They have the discipline and the work ethic to do the right thing whether or not someone's looking, even if it requires sacrifice.

Chapter 13

Be in the Gray Zone

as told by Marc Blaushild

My father has often said Famous is not a black and white organization, nor is it a place for people who think in absolutes. He says, "Many companies that have failed are black and white. Their people will say, 'We can't do this' or 'we're not allowed to do that.' Anyone can live in a black and white organization because it's easy. People don't have to think critically because the policy makes the decision for them. But the company will probably fail because the world is gray. Twenty percent may be black or white, but the 80 percent in the middle will make or break the company because that's where empowered people get to do what they think is right."

Companies that keep too much decision-making power at the top will fail. We empower leaders in all areas of our organization to collaborate rather than keeping all decision-making authority in the corporate office.

Associates have to know the processes, procedures and guidelines of their role, but we don't have a policy that dictates what to do in every situation. As long as our actions and decisions are legal, ethical and moral, our business is about doing what needs to be done to serve customers.

When people ask me, "What should I do?" I try to respond, "What do you think we should do?" Or, "If you were me, what would you say?" Most of the time we aren't deciding between right and wrong. We have different paths we can take, and we have to decide which is most aligned with our Purpose, Fundamentals and goals.

Many years ago, I asked an executive at a billion-dollar company, "How did you get here?"

He said, "I had to learn how to intelligently violate company policy."

The gray area my dad talks about is where we empower our team to do what's right for our customers and our business. It's where we trust them to make the right decisions for the company and our customers, even if we have to "intelligently violate company policy".

Here's a great example from John Palermo that illustrates why black and white rules don't work so well in our business:

"I was an assistant manager at Akron, and we had a policy in place that customers had to have a receipt to return a product. Our customer, Bob, came in with a return, and we had a counter guy who said, 'Well, to return this, we need your receipt.'

Bob explained, 'Well, you sent me the wrong items so what my receipt says is not what I received. I'm bringing it back to you, and I want credit on what you were supposed to send me.'

They got into an argument because of this policy. Bob was 6 feet 4 inches tall and about 280 pounds, so when I heard him raise his voice from my office around the corner, I ran out there. I asked, 'Bob, what's the problem?' Bob then explained what happened. I looked at the associate and said, 'Let's take care of Bob and process his credit. We didn't even send him the right stuff.'

That sales associate was a black-and-white person. If you give a black-and-white person a policy, they will live (and die) by it. They'll also be the first ones to point the finger and say, "It's not my fault; it's this person over here who made the policy."

You see policies in retail, like a 30-day return policy. Because it's a transactional business, they hold true to those rules. Because our company's success is rooted in long-term relationships where every interaction matters, policies don't always work so well.

We prefer guidelines because guidelines consider the circumstances. We make mistakes; customers make mistakes. We might send the wrong product; they might order the wrong product. We understand that neither side is perfect in this relationship, so when someone makes a mistake, we make things right rather than following policy. The associate must make a decision within the guidelines to keep the customer happy.

They need to work with customers to solve problems, even pushing the guidelines if it's in the customer's best interests. Whether it's waiving a shipping charge or working with a vendor to give a customer credit when they don't have to, we win in the long-term if it's the right thing to do."

When we consistently make decisions that reflect our Core Values and Fundamentals, we'll earn people's trust and be successful in the long run. We take extreme care to find and foster people who reflect those values and practice those behaviors.

"We have to be very selective of who we hire to make sure we're bringing in individuals who already have a good foundation of the Core Values and Fundamentals," Kevin says.

In a gray environment, the right decision may cost the company more time or money. But we don't think in terms of one-time costs. We think about our long-term relationship with the customer who will remember what we did to serve them long after that one-time cost is paid. They will trust us because they know we always act on their behalf.

"My favorite expression is 'you can win the battle and lose the war,'" my dad says. "You could win the battle on that situation, but the 'war' is trust and goodwill with the customer. People will argue about saving nickels and dollars, but when you have a customer that might spend $50,000 or $100,000 per year you have to keep perspective. If you keep their trust by working on their behalf, customers will reward you with their business for years thereafter. But if you lose the trust, you lose the customer forever."

What's right for the customer is usually right for our business. That's how we make decisions in the gray zone, whether from the boardroom or from the branch counter.

Chapter 14

Learning from Mistakes

as told by Marc Blaushild

Look at this list and guess what it represents:

    Mickey Mantle (17)
    Willie Mays (14)
    Ted Williams (10)
    Alex Rodriguez (10)
    Roberto Clemente (9)
    Reggie Jackson (9)
    Ryne Sandberg (9)
    Mark McGwire (9)

If you're a baseball fan, you'll instantly recognize these famous players and, like me, you might assume this list has something to do with great performances at bat. What stunned me was that this list represents players with the most strikeouts in All-Star Games.

This list shows that to succeed at the highest level, you must take swings that sometimes fail. If these players hadn't been so successful, they wouldn't have made it to All-Star Games, wouldn't have had more at bats in those games and wouldn't have "failed" so many times. They had more opportunities to swing the bat, which led to more hits, and strikeouts.

At Famous, we trust our associates to swing the bat and make decisions that serve our customers, benefit our company and fulfill our purpose. We don't expect people to have a perfect batting average. Mistakes will happen when you swing, and strikeouts provide valuable experience and lessons that help improve your game. The best players learn from their mistakes to play better next time.

"I used to get upset when we made a mistake," Jay says. "We might have screwed up a delivery, and I'd get all worked up. My father didn't laugh much, but he would laugh at my frustration. He'd say, 'It's a good thing we made a mistake.' I'd ask, 'Why is it a good thing to make a mistake?' He replied, 'Because we will correct mistakes immediately, when many of our competitors don't correct mistakes.'"

Hyman may not be around anymore to laugh at our frustration, but we still remind our associates to find opportunities for improvement in each mistake, just as he did. It's a lesson that still sticks in Randy Patton's mind, nearly 40 years after joining Famous.

"I'll never forget meeting Marc and Jay early on. After they brought me into Famous they said, 'We want you to run the purchasing department.' Marc sat there and said 'Randy, don't be afraid to make a mistake because it's one of the best ways you can learn.'

It still sticks in my mind because I'm thinking, 'These folks have a lot of trust in me!' Keep in mind, I could write a purchase order and spend $1 million at the drop of a hat. It was staggering. At the time I managed more than $100 million in spend and they said, 'Don't be afraid to make a mistake.' It instilled a lot of confidence. Because of the attitude from management I'd always say to our Purchasing team, 'Don't be afraid to make a mistake because that's how you learn.'

When you give associates freedom to make decisions in gray areas, you must support them if their decisions aren't successful.

"If you give associates that freedom, you better have their back if they make a mistake," John Palermo says. "If they had good intentions but made a bad choice, I'll back them up every time and say, 'You did what you thought was right.'"

We put processes and accountability measures in place to prevent significant errors, but when you give associates responsibility, it requires balancing oversight with the freedom to roam the fields and learn by making mistakes.

Many organizations punish people for making mistakes. As a result, people keep quiet if they happen. But we know mistakes are far too valuable to ignore. We take advantage of these teachable moments and ask, "What have you learned?" We talk people through the situation to figure out what we will do to ensure this mistake doesn't happen again.

I've never heard my dad yell at an associate for making a mistake, and I can't imagine that my grandfather ever did, either. Some coaches get in players' faces when they come off the field after making a mistake, but we mark it down as an opportunity to get better.

"I can't think of any time we've ever gotten rid of somebody for making a bad decision," Brian, says. "People make mistakes. People make bad decisions. Everybody's human, so we're forgiving. We're willing to work with people and give them an opportunity to learn and improve.

"Sometimes companies give up on people too early and say, 'This person is not good at this job; let's get rid of them and find someone else.' It's our job to make sure someone is successful, so we'll do whatever we can to teach and work with people."

Stephen Covey says, "We judge ourselves by our intentions and others by their actions." What if we judged ourselves by our actions and others by their intentions? At Famous, we believe people are intrinsically good and want to do what's right. There will be strikeouts as we swing the bat. It's our responsibility as leaders to coach associates and treat mistakes as part of the growth and development process. By working through problems together and improving instead of placing blame, we build loyalty with our associates, vendors and customers.

COMMUNICATION

Chapter 15

Technology Transformation
as told by Marc Blaushild

Communication is vital to our collective success. We work hard to always be transparent with our team and "share the why." When you're steering an organization, it's crucial to communicate where we've been, where we are, where we're going, and how we're going to get there. That's how everyone moves in the same direction toward success. The more aligned we all are, the more we will work in unison to get things done.

When Hyman was building Famous, he had to walk around the office and travel to branches to communicate with associates. After telephones and fax machines arrived, my father still committed to physically traveling from branch to branch to have meaningful conversations. Today, we try to balance those face-to-face interactions with new technology that helps us stay in touch with associates and customers even faster. As the tools and technologies for communication evolve, we're constantly adapting, even when updating our technology means rethinking our entire operation. That's how critical communication is in business.

Communication has always been part of our culture at Famous. Though Hyman was a man of few words, he constantly communicated with the early Famous team. He was like a doctor making the rounds every evening to ask associates about their day. He did daily huddles before it was popular. Before everyone went home, they gathered to discuss their plans for the next day.

But in-person communication became more difficult as we grew. When my dad took over the company, there were too many people for him to communicate with one-on-one. He put regional managers in place and relied on them to convey messages across their network.

As the structure and size of the company evolve, we continue to adapt how we communicate as a team spread across a growing footprint.

I love talking with people who have worked at Famous for many decades and have experienced the technology transition. Tom Krejci joined Famous in 1970 and was a Branch Manager, Regional Manager and Marketing Director, among others. He remembers how we communicated about purchasing, inventory, pricing, and invoicing before all of this information was available in real-time on a computer screen. In Tom's words:

> *Everything used to be much more manual. Before we were connected electronically, there was a lot of paper and effort involved in communication. There was no such thing as a fax machine, a cell phone or voicemail. The phone rang, and it didn't stop ringing until you picked it up. If you wanted to get a quote to somebody, you had to get in your car, drive over and hand it to them.*
>
> *We had a Purchasing Agent back in those days, Johnny Kallos, and Johnny placed most of the company's orders. Every day, we did physical inventories at branches, and we reported them to Johnny, so he could calculate what we needed. We sent out purchase orders by U.S. Mail.*
>
> *We did pricing manually, too. Picture someone sitting behind a desk surrounded by a stack of books and price sheets. There could be 300 sections of different manufacturers to leaf through to find the price of each item. There might be 10, 16 or 25 items on an invoice, and this person had to price each one individually.*
>
> *There was different pricing between branches, so customers could call on the west side of Cleveland and get one price, and then call the east*

side of Cleveland and get a different one. We'd say, "We'll beat that price," but we were beating ourselves! Back then, when a customer had an account in Cleveland, and they picked something up from Akron or Canton or Columbus, we'd have to call Cleveland to figure out what their pricing was. Then, we had to put it on an inter-company ticket. It was mind-boggling and time-consuming.

Then they took that day's work and handed it to somebody else who would use an Addressograph machine. This machine would go "bah-BUMP, bah-BUMP, bah-BUMP," making all this noise all day long to print out invoices. After that, someone else had to record the orders into our accounting system. So, a day's work became a day-and-a-half because everything was manual.

In those days' manual was the only option, but by the time I joined the company in 1985, technology was outpacing Famous. We still hand-priced inventories, fed rolls of paper into bookkeeping machines, punched numbers into check-writing machines, and manually typed accounts receivable reports. We filled entire floors of buildings with filing cabinets and hired people to do nothing but file papers.

The fax machine was a game-changer for us. My father still gets excited remembering how instantaneous the technology was. It saved him from hand-typing multiple carbon copies of announcements to send each branch. It helped the branches communicate to the whole network more conveniently. When a branch ran short of certain products, it faxed a "want list" to the other branches requesting backup. Each branch received faxes from other branches every day requesting products.

During this time, I was leading our Famous Telephone division that sold telecommunications products, and we implemented state-of-the-art distribution technology. But at Famous, it would take days, a week or longer to determine where products were, and then move them around the company to get them to the customer. The size of our growing operation made this manual approach time consuming and cumbersome. As we entered the 1990s, we were running a $100-plus million wholesale business without computers. We knew we needed to change. We had to implement technology, or we would not survive.

When Johnny Kallos announced his retirement, I joined Famous Supply. Soon after, our team began the retirement of our manual approach. We decided it was finally time to adopt a computer system to transition Famous into modern times, and in 1998 we invested heavily in technology.

But how were we going to accomplish this initiative? How were we going to create the database? How were we going to build the infrastructure to support it? How were we going to implement it? How were we going to train people to use it? How were we going to think, act, and work differently? The answers to these questions all involved massive communication throughout a period of major change that lasted over five years.

Buy-in was relatively easy because we'd built trust with our team over many years. Most of our people had been expecting this change and understood we needed technology improvements to survive. Many of them were asking for a computer system as they saw what we were up against in the marketplace. They felt us falling behind competitors and knew how our manual way's slowed productivity and hurt customer service.

Once we acquired the software, we purchased over 400 new computers. We implemented the same Eclipse Enterprise Resource Planning (ERP) system from our telephone division to integrate our branches onto one unified system. We launched an e-commerce website to let customers check pricing and availability, place orders, and pay invoices online in real-time.

Rolling out technology required constant communication and training. In many cases, we were showing people how to use a computer for the first time before we could teach them how to use the software system. Some of our associates had never encountered technology because their job didn't demand it. It made a few people skeptical and apprehensive—nothing we couldn't solve with either communication or training.

Technology brought us up to speed just in time for the economy to crash again. The new millennium brought many challenges, between the Dot-com bubble bursting, recession raging and banks and businesses failing all around us. Tough economic times became a catalyst for us to look deeper than a new computer system and think differently about our entire approach to doing business. The world had changed, our customers had evolved and we, too, needed to transform if we wanted to continue serving them into the next century.

But our transformation wasn't just about transitioning from a manual company onto a computer system. This change enabled a complete overhaul of our organizational structure and the way we communicated and operated a business across a growing number of locations.

Chapter 16

Crystal Ball

as told by Marc Blaushild

Famous hired a consultant in 2001 to help our management team facilitate a strategic plan for the rocky economic climate. One afternoon, the consultant sat down in my office and gave me my first assignment.

"Pretend you fell asleep and woke five years later," he said. "What would you want the company to look like when you woke up? What would be different?"

I went home that night and wrote, collecting my thoughts and reflecting on conversations I shared with dozens of our associates and industry peers throughout time. I thought about the differences between our telephone supply business and our building supply business (HVAC, Plumbing, Industrial and Building Products). I thought about the tumultuous economic environment around us. I wrote about the opportunities and challenges I saw on our path to becoming a stronger, healthier and more profitable company. I wrote about the priorities we'd need to focus on in the coming years. I wrote about the ways our leadership, our management and our associates would all have to think and act differently (including me) to achieve the results we envisioned for the future.

MERGING TO A SINGLE P&L

As Famous added locations and acquired other wholesalers throughout the years, we gave each of them the autonomy to manage its own inventory, pricing structure, customer base, and ultimately, its own profitability. Essentially, each branch operated as its own separate business. Although branches stayed in alignment with our overall values and expectations, there were differences, and even competition, among them.

We talked about teamwork and tried to empower associates who had positive intentions of helping customers. But our operational structure and incentive programs were not aligned. Branches battled against one another, creating competition instead of collaboration to help "our" local customers.

As technology and logistics evolved, customers broadened their bases and expanded their markets. They now went to multiple Famous branches, and our structure wasn't facilitating the teamwork required to serve customer needs seamlessly in the new millennium. John Palermo describes the tension this caused:

"A lot of branches, even the managers, were in direct competition with each other. Our sister companies, J.F. Good and Pittsburgh Plumbing, were as competitive between each other as they were with other wholesalers in the market, even though we were part of the same company. There was a protective mindset that evolved. It was Pittsburgh Plumbing versus J.F. Good versus Famous, between branches and between companies under the same umbrella. We talked team, but we didn't fully live team. Neighboring branches were at battle. We competed for the same business. Sometimes, we competed for the same customers and it became adversarial. Every warehouse looked at the want list faxes from all the other branches and associates walked around to see if they had the items. Beyond that, there was no guarantee that branches would send the material other branches requested."

People felt the effects of our segmented branch structure throughout the organization, and we had to restructure. We had to become one team, unified against external competition, with a single scoreboard tracking our performance.

The first priority I wrote about when I looked five years ahead in my crystal ball was to see Famous unified as a single team, sharing profits through a single P&L. This is what I wrote:

"We absolutely cannot have division among our people, management, departments, branches, regions, or at corporate. It needs to be a 'given' that we will have total teamwork, and nothing less. Only team players will be allowed to stay within the organization. Those that cannot get on board with this philosophy will be asked (helped) to leave the company. In order for this philosophy to work, we need a different mindset. To get everyone to make decisions that are always in the best interest of the overall company, we need to implement a 'global profit sharing' program. We will win or lose as a team. This means that all associates receive the same Team Bonus (as a percentage of their base pay) based on our overall company performance.

The long-term impact of this will benefit our associates, customers, vendors, and all stakeholders. We will share resources (technical, sales, corporate, physical assets, etc.) between branches so we may provide the best quality service in our industry. We will not be consumed with what branch gets credit for a sale or who absorbed the cost, but rather with how to best serve one another and our customers with speed and agility."

Transforming Famous from individual profit centers into a centralized operation with one P&L and balance sheet was a monumental change. We discussed the concept in management team meetings before making a final decision, then built cross-functional teams to involve various perspectives across the organization. A change this big wasn't a matter of flipping a switch. We needed a strong foundation of communication, teamwork and buy-in to get everyone on board.

Communicating constantly and transparently, we explained the benefits of a Team Bonus where all associates would share in the company's profits when we exceed our corporate financial benchmarks as one team. We worked to convince people that focusing our efforts and resources on a common goal, rather than competing ones, would take us all farther and result in a larger

Team Bonus. About 90 percent bought into our new focus immediately, while the rest took a some convincing before they either got on board or left the company.

Gradually, we integrated branch operations into a unified system. We centralized core functions by promoting key leaders in areas such as sales, operations and purchasing that were previously the responsibility of each respective branch. We reorganized our sales process to leverage resources and expertise throughout the company. We moved away from commission-based pay and put all outside sales associates on salary, which is not traditional in wholesale distribution.

This was a tremendous shift in our operational and financial structure, and it required a tremendous amount of planning. This change would eventually cause ripples (and some waves) that revolutionized our culture.

SHIFTING CULTURE OF PROFIT SHARING

I remember reading an article Jim Collins wrote a decade before his book Good to Great came out. He said that business strategy can change immediately based on its customer's needs or market conditions. However, Core Values are unwavering and stand the test of time.

The culture of a company is somewhere in between the often-changing strategy and the always-steady values, Collins wrote. Culture should gradually adapt to the times, but it won't happen in a day. It's like a ship slowly turning to shift course. If you wait too long to make cultural adjustments, you may veer off course and crash or sink.

To steer Famous toward success in challenging times, we adjusted our strategy. This shift required changing our organizational structure, which had a massive impact on our culture. Because our values remained steady, it gave our associates comfort in knowing we weren't turning into a different Famous, but rather a new, improved Famous.

As we communicated this new vision throughout the company, it gained momentum. Key players on our multifunctional teams communicated the vision to the associates around them. Our people drove the change. It wasn't just pushed down from corporate, so it gained traction.

When skeptics saw the results of cooperation, they realized what we could achieve by working together. The adage of two heads being better than one rang true. In our case, we had over 20 branches with hundreds of people changing the way they worked and interacted to get on the same page. It took some years for the company to change our collective mindset and slowly grow from competitive, to cooperative, to collaborative.

"Before Marc led that change, things were a little cutthroat," says Dave Figuly. "Branches didn't like to give up an account or an order. There was good teamwork within branches, but not between branches. When we changed to universal profit-sharing, and then the year-end Team Bonus, it changed everyone's thinking. We are more of a team. We don't point fingers; we're all working together to get the same thing."

What was most encouraging during this period of change was how our team worked together to overcome the challenges. The people that fit our Core Values understood the changes were to strengthen the teamwork necessary to achieve more together than we ever could separately.

Instead of trying to protect inventory, expertise and accounts at each location, branches started to work together to deliver the best we could collectively offer to our customers.

SHARING RESOURCES TO ACHIEVE MORE TOGETHER

In an industry where individual achievement and commissions are the norm, becoming one team with shared resources and fair rewards gave us a huge advantage. John Palermo explains:

"As great as our outside sales associates are, there's no way that an outside sales associate can be an expert in every category because of the wide range of products we have. The most important thing I tell outside sales associates is to focus on face time with the customer. Their job is about building strong relationships and understanding customers' needs and challenges. We don't need them writing up orders or doing quotes because we have resources and support teams to do that in every product category.

If you're a commission-based company a lot of individuals are working almost like sub-contractors. Many of them might be reluctant to ask coworkers for support because they don't want to share their commission. When a company works together as an organization without team members worrying about who's receiving recognition or commission, people will naturally work together."

Under our previous structure, District Sales Managers were responsible for the results of their respective regions. This meant each one tried to master a wide scope of product categories, from HVAC to plumbing to processed piping, to sell as much as we could to a variety of customers across one region. In our new structure, they were still responsible for customers within their territories, and now had more incentive to leverage company-wide resources such as product specialists with specific expertise.

One customer might work with three associates for a single account: one to handle the HVAC, another for plumbing and a third for hydronics. We could have three sales reps working on one major account, and we win the business because our salespeople will bring in expertise the customer needs. That rarely happens in individual, commission-based profit centers.

One of our greatest success stories involves long-time outside sales associate, Mike Scott. Mike is one of our best "hunters", an expert at bringing on new business. Over many years he established an account base that did $8 million in yearly revenue. We sat down with him and asked him to give away $1 to $2 million to other outside salespeople who could maintain and service the accounts he's solidified so that he could do what he does best—bring in new business. As we moved accounts from him to others, and lowered the sales revenue he managed, we gave him a raise because he made a decision that made Famous a better, more profitable company. With the extra time, he's been able to bring on even more new business.

Restructuring Famous into a profit-sharing team was a monumental change that took several years of heavy lifting and another few years of tweaks and adjustments. Structurally, strategically and culturally, we would never be the same.

Chapter 17

The Third Generation

as told by Jay Blaushild

When Marc came into the company, I didn't put him in a corner office with a nice title the way many of my friends did with their kids when they joined their family's business. Instead, I put him at the ground-level of a small company we owned at the time called Famous Telephone Supply.

Marc started in the warehouse. He swept floors, received product on the shipping dock, stocked shelves, pulled orders, and loaded trucks. After his time in the warehouse, he worked in purchasing, credit, marketing, and sales. It wasn't until after he had experienced all of those roles that I made him General Manager of the Telephone division. Because the company was smaller than Famous Supply, he had his hands in every function of the company and could learn every aspect of the distribution business.

Revenues at Famous Telephone doubled during the time Marc led the business, going from $10 million to $20 million. We ended up selling that business because it didn't fit with our core focus of building materials, but many people came back to Famous years later because they wanted to work with Marc and the rest of the associates they knew. The company performed well, and Marc showed poise. He proved, without a doubt, that he had the ability to run Famous.

Marc has done things for Famous that I never could have done, such as the Team Bonus, our unified distribution model and our 40 Fundamentals.

A problem leaders often have is to want the people they lead to do things the way they would do it. One of my dad's favorite expressions was:

"You can't put your head on their shoulders."

No one can impose their style on anyone else. Marc does things his way, and we're all blessed for it.

Massive changes were transforming Famous in the early 2000s, so I decided it was time for the company to officially step into the next generation. In 2004, I promoted Marc to President of Famous Enterprises, except I didn't tell him about it before I did it. I announced it at a customer appreciation event in front of 500 people, both customers and associates. I had been grooming him for leadership, but he had no idea I was planning to make that announcement when I did.

I blindsided him again when I named him CEO at our annual trade show (called our "Expo") in 2007, in front of several hundred associates, customers and suppliers.

John Palermo remembers:

"Most of us were waiting for the change to come. The business had become segmented over time as we acquired companies and opened new branches. A lot of people weren't aligned with the business, and someone had to tie everything back together. I think Jay understood that Marc was more capable of doing that than he was, and that's why he stepped back. It was the right time. Marc had a vision of what he knew the company could become, but we needed to get it out of the '60s. We were already in the next century, but not running the business accordingly. Marc knew what changes to make and Jay understood it was time to let go.

I give Jay a lot of credit because he let Marc transform and evolve the business. We kept moving forward, and Jay's support encouraged us to get behind the changes and keep on pushing as a team."

Rick Sonkin says:

"I've always been impressed with the fact that once Jay turned over the reins to Marc, he let Marc be the leader. He allowed Marc to make decisions and be front and center. In a lot of family businesses I'm involved with, the transition of control is a difficult thing for high-functioning CEOs. It's hard for them to have the self-awareness to know their time is better served overseeing the business as a Chairman than operating it. It's a tribute to Jay, and it allows Marc to accomplish more in his role. And Marc is now doing the same thing with Brian and Kevin, and the rest of Executive Leadership Team. As they develop, and the company grows, he empowers them with more autonomy and responsibility."

Chapter 18

The Heart of the Operation

as told by Marc Blaushild

Famous finally had the people and the technology in place for us to collaborate effectively to serve customers. But we still had to reduce the time it took to move products around the company. We knew our business was growing faster than our distribution network could support, and we had to move to a better, more efficient system.

If our new ERP system is like the brain of our business that stores and processes data and information, distribution is the heart that pumps products to where they're needed. At the turn of the millennium, we knew we needed a heart transplant. The next key investment in our transformation was centralizing our purchasing, distribution and logistics from 2002 to 2005.

In my five-year crystal ball vision, I wrote:

"What our customers need more than anything is timely, accurate, quality service. To accomplish this, a new stocking, trucking and logistics system is required. Our customers cannot afford to wait three-to-10 days to receive material after they place their order. They shouldn't pay for distributor inefficiencies related to excess inventory, duplicate handling or damaged material.

We will have a Central Distribution Center with same-day, next-day or two-day delivery to customers and Famous branches. All trucks will commit to deliver next day to every branch from the Central Distribution Center, regardless of the size of the load. This will allow the sales department to sell with confidence of accurate shipments, high fill rates and timely deliveries.

The centralized purchasing team will ensure that the right inventory is in the right places, in the right quantities, and turning. They will communicate with marketing and sales, and we will be a true link in the supply chain from our suppliers to the customer."

By bringing together our talented people and new technologies, we built cross-functional teams to plan and implement a centralized and integrated purchasing and distribution system. Our electronic warehouse management software tracked where products were, how many we had in stock, when and where they sold, and more, giving us a new visibility and understanding of our inventory.

CENTRALIZED PURCHASING WITH DECENTRALIZED INPUT

To centralize our purchasing operation, we had to replace our Vice President of Purchasing, and 50-year Famous veteran, John Kallos, who had recently retired. We called Randy Patton, who had led Purchasing at J.F. Good before Famous acquired it. We asked Randy to come back and lead a team of people to steer the difficult transition. Randy remembers:

"It was a challenge, and it took time. What we were doing was taking a lot of the decision-making power out of the branch locations and saying, 'Based on the data, this is the inventory you should have, and this is the price you should sell it at'.

Figuring out how to get the right products at the right place at the right time was, and still is, a challenge. But we worked hard to build confidence with our team. I spent months traveling to all of our locations to educate, build trust and evaluate inventories. After, we'd invite all the people in the branch out to dinner and have what we called a communication roundtable. We'd ask, 'What's working for you and what's not working? How can we improve it? What kinds of things do you need that we don't see?'

Centralized software took a burden off of our associates in purchasing and inventory management, but it didn't remove them from the equation.

We needed to pair data with insight from our team members to serve customers at a high level. Customer-facing associates in the branches have a unique perspective of what local customers need that our warehouse management system can't replicate. We had people from the branches help with the transition so that people who these changes affected were represented at the table. From the start, we encouraged associates to collaborate with the purchasing group as much as possible."

With our new inventory management system in place, we were ready to enhance our distribution capability. In February 2003, we hired our first Director of Distribution, Tanja Kozul, who had distribution center and logistics experience with a multibillion-dollar office supply company. She joined Famous during a turbulent time of change, which is actually what attracted her to Famous. According to Tanja:

"Famous brought me in to work on the team that was designing the Central Distribution Center. I could tell that Famous operated a certain way for many decades. Marc was just looking at the company and creating the vision for how the business would look in 20 years. They were taking Famous into the next era and strategically positioning the business to become a larger player in its markets.

Many family-owned companies get passed to the next generation and continue operating their business as is. Marc put in the investment to make significant changes, and, more importantly, he involved the people to orchestrate the changes. That commitment keeps people here and engaged."

Soon after, we were receiving products at our new 350,000 square-foot Central Distribution Center in Sebring, Ohio. The mountains of furnaces, air conditioners and water heaters were breathtaking. In March 2005, the Central Distribution Center (CDC) officially began working 24/7 to supply every branch in the company with products, every day.

We built a team of drivers to operate 17 tractor-trailers, and additional flatbeds to deliver pipe, sheet metal, commercial HVAC rooftops, and other large items. This evolved our intra-company transfer system, which began in 1988 with one 1970 International tractor that hauled a 40-foot trailer and logged more than one million miles!

THE HEART OF THE OPERATION

With an integrated ERP system, a reorganized operational structure and a centralized distribution model, Famous could better serve our customers, true to my great-grandfather's purpose. Through the hard work of countless associates, we positioned ourselves to deliver on our promise of Famous service.

Even with all the changes that took place in 2005, we beat every sales projection for the year. Most branches ended the year with record-setting sales numbers. Our accomplishments directly resulted from associates working together, bound by the shared goal of giving our customers exceptional service.

Chapter 19

A Different Way of Communicating

as told by Marc Blaushild

The first move my father made when he took over the company in 1970 was to put Regional Managers in place to help him manage and lead the business. Similarly, one of my first initiatives as President was to overhaul our corporate communication practices to keep our sprawling network of diverse branches better connected as we continued to grow.

Before email, webinars and other broadcasting mediums were invented, my dad spoke with numerous people and relied on individuals to deliver messages throughout the company. As we grew, an increasing number of people reported directly to him and communicating became time consuming.

When I stepped into the role, the company we had grown to over 500 associates. New technologies emerged that allowed us to communicative more efficiently, and it was no longer effective me to spend my time talking with a few key people, and hope the message spread to everyone else. I did, and still do, spend quality time with my direct reports and many other key associates. However, I didn't want to rely on that method for the most important communications that needed to cascade to the entire company.

We needed more people directly involved in the communication. I wanted more people to hear my message directly from me, and I wanted to hear from more people before we made strategic decisions for the company.

This communication overhaul began with good, old-fashioned, face-to-face chats. In 2005, our management team made the rounds to visit every branch location for "Lunch, Listen and Learn" meetings with all of our associates. The purpose was twofold: first, to communicate the changes associated with our new organizational structure, our single P&L and streamlined distribution model, in an open forum. Second, I wanted to hear what people needed from us to implement those changes, and any other ideas they had. We wanted to show that effective communication flows every way, not just from the "top-down", and that everyone has a voice in sharing ideas and opinions.

Building upon the trust we had worked to establish throughout our history, we evolved our culture of open and honest communication.

OPEN-DOOR LEADERSHIP

An important decision we made when I first stepped into my role was instituting an Open-Door Policy. If you walked into the old Famous corporate office at the corner of North Union and Perkins streets in Akron, Ohio, you would've seen the example I tried to set for the rest of the business. Instead of a corner office tucked away from the traffic of associates, suppliers, customers, and other guests, my office was located right off of the main lobby, next to the reception desk and impossible to miss. A second door to my office opened directly into the mail room behind the reception desk, so it became a convenient shortcut for associates who opted to cut through my office instead of walking around the large reception area to get their mail. After all, the doors were, literally, always open.

Of course, the goal of our open-door policy is not to provide a shortcut to the mailroom. I wanted to show that my time and attention is not off-limits to anyone, at any time, for any reason. My hope was that associates would not be afraid to walk in (or through) to share what was on their minds. In many organizations, it might terrify people to walk into the CEO's office. But Famous has been working for generations to build a trusting, family-life environment where everyone has a voice, and open office doors emphasize that. Kevin, says:

"I don't think people look at my dad as the big, scary CEO. We try to build a comfort level where, regardless of your role, everyone has a voice. When Brian and I were younger, our parents taught us to value everyone's perspective. When my dad coached our teams, he was equally likely to strike up a conversation with a coach, someone in maintenance or the principal. You feel that throughout the company. People know we'll listen to their feedback and follow through to address it. Everyone has something to contribute, and we always try to practice that no matter their role or job title. The best ideas should always win."

Because of this environment, our communication style is casual, like talking with a friend or someone in your family. It can be easier for me because when I'm here I often am talking with someone from my family! But we work to create the same feeling for everyone. The tone of conversations in meetings or inside branches is the opposite of "stuffy". We share jokes, laughs and have fun, all while having meaningful discussions to move the business forward.

Building meaningful relationships with coworkers is just as important to us as doing the work. The time we spend getting to know one another what builds teamwork and trust. The work still gets done, and the quality of work is better because people are working together and enjoying what they're doing.

The atmosphere of trust and open communication doesn't just come from my office. It mostly comes from the warm, approachable people in our Famous Family. Walk through a branch, distribution center or our corporate headquarters and you'll be hard-pressed to find a closed office door. Unless someone needs privacy for a call or meeting, the doors are open.

"None of us sit in our offices with doors closed," Pete Bastulli says. "I know it may sound gimmicky, but that sets the tone. We take the open-door policy seriously, and we're always accessible. I like to say my cell phone is like Denny's—it's always open, always close by. That's a significant aspect of fostering a culture of open communication."

Our associates know they can call anyone on our management team, at any time. They can pop into my office, pick up the phone or request a meeting on my calendar. I'm always open to sitting down with an associate to listen to their thoughts or discuss their ideas.

I never want to go around our managers' heads, though, so I may redirect associates through the proper chain. This is how John Palermo explains it to new associates:

"Even with open doors, associates still have to follow protocol within the organization. If a sales associate has an issue and goes right to Marc Blaushild, they never give their manager the opportunity to address it. That's not open door. Associates have to give leaders an opportunity to do the right thing before going around them. If they still feel uncomfortable with a decision, it's okay to step it up. I tell my direct reports, 'If I give you direction and you don't believe in it, talk to me about it. If we still disagree, and you think it goes against the company strategy, direction or culture, we can talk to Marc.' At that point, I won't get upset because we're not always going to agree. First, we try to resolve it and gain consensus on what the right thing to do is. If that doesn't succeed, we've built a process to take disagreements through the company, instead of going over somebody's head."

Our open-door policy also extends to customers. We publish a customer service guide for our customers, listing the names, phone numbers and email addresses of our leaders, Product Specialists and other contacts throughout the company. Our support teams and leaders are always accessible to customers and suppliers, so they know Famous service is a phone call away.

To stand behind that policy, we never screen our phone calls. When customers call in, we don't ask who it is, so we can get permission to forward their call. Customers know they can walk into a branch or headquarters and talk to anyone, for any reason that's important to them.

OPEN-BOOK MANAGEMENT

Our communication style at Famous extends from the open door to open book. Not only are we accessible to hear feedback from associates, but we proactively communicate information to them.

We often compare Famous to a sports team. Teams can't reach peak performance without knowing the score. As important as it is to make sure we're all running the same play, it's just as important to keep an eye on the scoreboard and review the game film to see where we need to improve.

The distribution industry, much like sports, is a game of statistics. We're always measuring how well we Execute the Perfect Order; did we have the inventory the customer needed? Did we enter the order correctly? Was it picked, packed and shipped correctly? Did the shipment arrive on-time? Was any product damaged? Did we invoice it correctly? How well is our inventory turning?

With that mindset, I wanted every Famous associate to see and understand our financial data. I wrote about this in my five-year crystal ball, envisioning that everyone would have access to monthly P&L information in easy-to-understand formats that tracked our performance against goals and previous periods.

In 2007, I started quarterly conference calls for all associates to share financial results, communicate our strategy and tell stories of culture, leadership and our Core Values in action. In 2009, it became a monthly call. To this day, all associates attend every month's call.

Before the calls began, we provided financial training to all associates and taught them how to interpret the information we were sharing.

Two special people drove this initiative. The first was Curt Brown, our former CFO. He was with Famous for just 38 months, but it seemed like 38 years. Tragically, he had a heart attack and passed away in 2011. He was brilliant, warmed our people's hearts and minds, and was instrumental in helping our team better understand the financial aspect of the distribution business. The second was, now former, Famous Advisory Board member, Brent Grover. Brent is a wholesale distribution icon who has written acclaimed books, given numerous keynote speeches and consulted a wide variety of successful companies.

The information we share on these calls is to engage associates in two main topics; how we're performing financially and operationally, and our strategy for the company. My goal is to share where we stand, highlight what brought us this far and point out where we can improve. If I announce that we're making an investment in equipment or a new facility, I'll explain why we're doing it, how it will benefit associates and customers, and what we believe the impact will be for the company.

To close the call, I address questions associates have submitted in advance. I don't dodge any topics or choose which ones I want to answer; I cover 100 percent of the questions that come in. The questions come in through my assistant and I receive them anonymously. I've never asked who submitted a question because some may have a negative tone, and I want them to keep flowing in. I estimate I've answered approximately 500 questions since we began the calls.

After the questions I share a "final thought" to leave associates with a takeaway to keep at the top of their mind. The hope is that this message sparks continued dialog around the company through 1-2-1s, departmental and branch meetings.

The challenge for me is delivering a 45-minute message to more than 700 people who range from managers with decades of Famous experience, to new associates in entry level roles.

I came to accept that a message that's elementary to one person may be complicated to another. I rely on our people to help mentor their fellow associates and interpret the communication throughout the company.

It's difficult to deliver one message to hundreds of people and make sure it resonates with everyone. We put these calls together, so our associates can understand our company goals and how those goals connect with their individual roles. Continued open door and open book management is how we'll achieve success as a company because it aligns with our Core Values and Fundamentals.

What I'm most proud of is that my sons, Brian and Kevin, now join me in this monthly communication. We've evolved from a conference call to a live video conference, and the three of us take turns sharing information throughout the 45-minute presentation. Brian handles most of the financial information, Kevin delivers the operating performance and we all share strategy, recognition and other meaningful stories that reflect our culture.

Chapter 20

Listening for Better Decisions
as told by Marc Blaushild

When I became President, we introduced company newsletters and conference calls to improve how our leadership communicated information up, down and across the organization. But great communication isn't just delivering messages. Communication revolves around listening, and listening is much more than just hearing what's said. True listening means taking the time to understand another person's perspective.

Effective communication revolves around leaders who keep their doors open, their words welcoming and their ears to the ground to encourage a free flow of thoughts and ideas. The feedback that leaders hear and sense from conversations and observations (especially nonverbal cues) shape the decisions we make. After communicating those decisions to the company, they should go right back to listening to assess whether it's working. And if it's not, that's okay, as long as we go back and adjust.

We all learn more when we listen before we speak. Sometimes we assume we know the right answer and jump into action. But when leaders slow down and listen to their people, they often find there's a better way to accomplish a goal than what they initially had in mind. So, the bigger, more strategic the decision is, the more time and energy we spend listening to our people to make sure we get it right.

"Years ago, we made decisions with fewer people around the table, maybe four or five," my dad says. "Today, we do it the right way. We involve many more people, and we listen. It's more time-consuming and the differences of opinion can be frustrating, but we get better answers because we get to more perspectives. More importantly, when people are involved in the decision-making process, they understand it and are better able to support it."

When we make strategic decisions like adopting new technology, investing in a Regional Distribution Center or moving our corporate headquarters, there isn't time for me to ask every associate what they think, so I have to rely on our Leadership Team to funnel feedback from their teams. I make it clear that I don't want them showing up to management meetings with only their own opinions; I want them to form their opinions based on what their people have shared with them. If we're discussing a sales strategy, I'm counting on our John Palermo to present an opinion that's based on feedback from his District Sales Managers, whose opinions are based on listening to their direct reports, who have listened to our customers.

We try to tackle decisions from every angle by working through as many perspectives as possible. We ask questions such as: Does this fit our Core Values and culture? Is this right for our people? How would it impact each functional area? Do we have the capability, resources, and the skill-set to do this? How would it affect customers? Is the timing right? How would this work financially; can we afford it? What roadblocks or fallout could we face? Are there unintended consequences we're missing? And, most importantly, is this what's best for Famous Enterprises? If we can answer those questions with clarity and consensus, we usually make the right decisions. One quote we often refer to is, "don't argue about who is right, discuss what is right for the business".

We can't hold anything back from each other. There are no wrong opinions and no bad ideas. If we're open-minded and respectful, every opinion or idea is an opportunity to springboard into something better until we land on the best decision.

If I sense any hesitation, silence or uneasy body language while discussing a big decision with the Leadership Team, I dig deeper to probe it out of them. We can't have associates hold their thoughts in, then go to the water cooler after the meeting and have private conversations with coworkers about how they really feel. We tell our people to bring the water cooler into the meeting. We want to put everything on the table, bring up every angle and hammer it out together.

When we come into areas of disagreement, I first remind everyone that our responsibility is to decide that's in the best interest of Famous Enterprises; not a particular functional area, district, branch, etc. We want our people to have pride, conviction and personal responsibility for their areas, but we also want them to leave their egos at the door, so we can work toward the best interests of our entire enterprise.

Sometimes, the most heated discussions can be the best way to land on the right decision. In the words of John Palermo:

"When you have open communication, there will be conflict. As a Leadership Team, we're responsible for deciding for over 700 associates, and if we make poor decisions, it will affect our people, our customers or the Team Bonus. It's not about winning or losing an argument. It's about figuring out what's best for the company. It's about those 700-plus people and their families. If I'm saying something, it's never meant to be disrespectful; it's said because I believe it's the right thing for the business. I tell my team, 'If you disagree with me, speak up and challenge the direction I'm going. You have to. If you don't, you're not helping me grow and you're not helping the company progress.'

Jay and I battled constantly, just like my father and I battled constantly. But I respected my father, and I respect Jay tremendously. Jay built an incredible business, but that doesn't mean he was always right. He'll tell you he knows he's not always right, and Marc will do the same. And now Brian and Kevin share that philosophy. The last thing they need is a bunch of yes-people running around. That's not beneficial to anyone.

Marc and I agree on about 90 percent of what we discuss. When we disagree, I end up agreeing with him on some, and he ends up agreeing with me on others. Sometimes we walk away from the table without ever agreeing, but we still move forward together. We still walk out of the room in consensus and as friends with mutual respect who support each other 100 percent. I remember leaving one meeting where we had been really going at it. It may have sounded bad to an outside observer, but really, it was a good thing. Those are positive examples because if we didn't believe in our direction, we would just roll over and play dead, and Marc wouldn't need any of us. But that's not who we are or what Famous is all about."

Famous associates are passionate. I remind everyone that having conviction for your role or functional area can't be at the expense of the rest of the company. Together, we have to be passionate about the success of Famous Enterprises, and our decisions have to support that.

If people are still arguing, I remind them of the moon rock.

Some years back, I heard former President Bill Clinton speak at Cuyahoga Community College on the East Side of Cleveland. He told us a story from his Presidency when he was in a meeting with the head of NASA and came across a moon rock. He asked to borrow it, keep it safe in the Oval Office and return it at the end of his term. He had a plan for this rock—and not as a paperweight. He planned to use it to build teamwork and collaboration.

Anytime a disagreement broke out in the Oval Office, President Clinton picked up the moon rock. He held it in the air, stared at it, and rubbed it until the people in the room stopped arguing to look at him, waiting for an explanation. When he caught everyone's attention, he said: "This rock is 3.6 billion years old, and we're only on Earth a short time. Let's put this in perspective. Can we work together to figure this out?" Inevitably, people would relax and come together to discuss the issue in a more civilized way.

When you keep the perspective of the bigger picture, it's easier to come to consensus and move forward in alignment. Regardless of how intense the discussion gets or how loud the debate is, our Leadership Team will come to an agreement. By the time we walk out the door, we will all support the decision and do our best to ensure it's successful.

TEAMWORK

Chapter 21

For the Common Good of the Team

as told by Marc Blaushild

I played a lot of competitive team sports growing up, but it was the team I coached in college that significantly shaped the way I think. My fraternity at Ohio State fought a decades-long rivalry with another fraternity across campus.

Every year, the freshman pledges who would be joining each fraternity battled out our rivalry on the football field. The faceoff drew crowds of hundreds, and the whole week was a big event leading up to this legendary, annual clash of two rivals. The week ended with a party at the winner's fraternity house.

I played the game as a freshman pledge, and our team won handily. I coached the pledge team during my junior year, and we won again. Our fraternity collectively asked that I remain coach my senior year, and the other team was gunning for us. We were fired up for the game, which was scheduled for a Thursday evening in the fall. We practiced for months leading up to the game.

The Monday before the game, everyone in our fraternity had dinner together. While we were eating, one of my fraternity brothers found me to share some news he had heard about our team's two best players. He told me he had heard through the grapevine that these two guys had no intention of joining our fraternity. They only wanted to play because the game garnered so much attention, and to go to the parties throughout the weekend. After the game, they planned on dropping out of the pledge class.

I immediately went directly to those two players, looked them straight in the eye and told them what I'd heard. I asked if it were true, and they admitted to me that they didn't plan on joining the fraternity. Without hesitation, I told them, "I appreciate your honesty. If you change your mind, you can still join the fraternity, but since you've told me this, you will not play in the game. So, it's your choice: You can leave the fraternity now, or practice with us and continue the process to join the fraternity, but you will not play."

They decided not to join, and at that moment we parted ways.

Shortly after this conversation ended, word spread to the rest of the fraternity. The house was split: half of the members agreed that our team should be about loyalty and supported the approach I took. The others were intent on winning the game and wondered how I could get rid of our two best players three nights before kickoff.

I explained that I would rather lose the game than have our team be anything but forthcoming with each other. I felt it was more important to do the right thing. I tried to act in the best interest of the fraternity, which is based on principles of brotherhood, loyalty and friendship, not boasting rights we might get if we won a football game.

The next day at practice we shifted people around to accommodate for the lost players. On top of that, one of our better players injured his ankle, and we had to move players around yet again, including our quarterback. We knew the opposing fraternity had recruited a strong team and were seeking revenge after our win the previous year. With our two best players out and another injured, some doubted we could pull off a win.

Most of the game on Thursday seemed to confirm what everyone feared, and we were losing 12-to-7 late in the fourth quarter. With about a minute left, we called a timeout and adjusted a play we had already run successfully three times prior. On our last drive, we ran the play with a small wrinkle; just enough to catch the other team off guard. We scored a touchdown and won the game 14-to-12. While I was proud of our players and the win, I would have rather lost the game without the two individuals who weren't in it for the team, than won the game with them.

I probably didn't realize it back then, but that was a defining moment in my life. I would rather work with loyal players who are committed to the team's goals than a talented player who's working to serve their ego. I haven't shared this story many times, but it illustrates the all-in level of teamwork we strive for at Famous. We don't want people on our team who are more focused on their personal goals than the team's success. Even if that hurts us in the short-term, it strengthens us in the long-term. We will only succeed if we foster a culture of teamwork.

In the distribution business, teamwork is not an option. It's a requirement. There are so many links in the supply chain that require a smooth handing off of the ball from one person to another until the customer gets the products they need. If anyone drops the ball, the chain breaks. If one part of the team fails, we all fail. Teamwork is one of our Core Values because it's critical to providing the quality of service our customers expect and need to run their businesses effectively.

When the phone rings at Famous, someone has to direct it to the proper person in the company. That person has to answer the customer's questions and bring in the right product specialists if the customer needs unique technical expertise. Then, a salesperson has to enter the customer's order accurately. Before any of this has happened, we need a buyer to anticipate the customer's product needs and purchase the right products to the right place, in the right quantities. When our vendor ships the product to us, we need someone in the warehouse to receive the material properly and put it away. When the time comes, another warehouse associate must pull the order accurately and stage it for pick-up or delivery. If it's going on a truck, someone has to load and secure the product correctly. Finally, it takes yet another person to deliver the order to the customer, damage-free and on time. Behind the scenes, someone else has to bill it correctly, and another to collect payment on time.

These basic "blocking and tackling" fundamentals are the foundation for our success. Although these tasks may appear relatively simple on the surface, to do them consistently well takes hard work, effort and focus. If we do everything right, but the order is entered incorrectly, we will fail the customer. We're only as strong as our weakest link. We can't win if 99 percent of us get their job done proficiently; it takes the entire team.

In order for a team to work together seamlessly, it requires that each player take personal responsibility for their role on the team. Every branch, functional area and individual at Famous is unique. On a football team, the kicker does something different than the wide receiver, and the left guard is not at all like the quarterback. But as different as they are, they each must perform their job successfully in order for the whole team will be successful.

Chapter 22

Recruiting Team Players
as told by Marc Blaushild

Hiring great people who fit our Famous Family culture has always been critical to our growth. My dad and grandfather were masters at asking the right questions to uncover whether a potential associate would live our values.

This is more important to us than a candidate's industry experience or how much revenue they might bring in. John Palermo remembers a specific hiring decision that illustrated this priority:

"I was looking for a sales associate and I interviewed a commission-based guy from a competitor who had reached out to us. He had a good reputation in the market, years of experience and a customer base that would bring in revenue. But when I heard him talk, it wasn't a lot of 'We'; it was all, 'I did this, I did that'. The great thing about our company is we don't have a lot of 'I's. We have a 'We' mentality. When I kept hearing, 'I,' it didn't feel right.

Marc asked how I was feeling about this person and I said, 'Marc, I know he could bring in revenue, but I'm really struggling on the cultural side.' Marc looked at me and said, 'John, I'd rather lose $2 million in revenue than hurt the culture of this company.' That made my decision easy, and we didn't bring him into the company."

During interviews, we listen for subtle indicators that reveal who the candidate truly is. Some people are good at saying what they think you want to hear, especially if they've done their research. It's important to dig in with thoughtful questions to understand if someone genuinely has the traits to be a contributing part of a cohesive team.

We're ultimately trying to answer these questions: Are they good people? Do they share our Core Values? Will they live the 40 Fundamentals? Are they talented people who will deliver results for the business? Hiring decisions are like picking teams in sports. It's important to know if they'll perform to our standards, and if they'll fit in the locker room.

You can learn a lot in an interview, but you won't truly understand people until they start the job. We take our time on the front-end and involve numerous people to draw a full assessment of a candidate's character and potential to produce results. After hiring, it's our job to assimilate new associates into the Famous Family and teach them the Famous Way. If they get off on the wrong foot, it's our responsibility.

To integrate people into the company, we bring our newest hires to a three-day New Associate Summit at our corporate office where they learn about our history and strategy, meet key leaders and see the whole scope of Famous. We talk in-depth about our Core Values, Fundamentals, operations, organizational structure, and goals.

The goal of the onboarding process is not just to teach new associates how Famous operates as a business. We show them what the Famous Family is and how we build relationships with each other and our customers. After all, that is how we operate as a business.

We attract people who are passionate about serving the customer, a skill-set that can't be taught. If they don't know HVAC, plumbing, industrial or building supplies, but are fanatics about serving people in whatever ways they can, they can learn the technical skills required to succeed. When those types of people enter the organization, our customer service aptitude multiplies and grows stronger.

In the early 1990s, we hired our first Director of Human Resources. Our management team narrowed the candidates to a final selection, and we were ready to make an offer to Norm Lawson, who had tremendous HR experience at a respected local company.

BECOMING FAMOUS

My father supported bringing on an HR leader, but first wanted to meet him. He called Norm and asked him to meet at the Bob Evans in Solon, Ohio, at 7:30 a.m. on a Saturday morning.

After a few hours of lively conversation, Norm excused himself at 10:30 a.m. to call his wife, Judy, and tell her he was still talking with Jay, and that he might be late for lunch. At 11:30 a.m., a new waitress from the next shift approached them both, asking if they'd like to order lunch. My dad said "yes." Norm excused himself again to call Judy and tell her she won't believe it, but Jay's still interviewing him, and he wouldn't be making it to lunch.

At 4:30 p.m., another waitress showed up and asked if they wanted to order dinner! Again, my father said "yes," and, again, Norm excused himself to call Judy. At this point, Judy can barely believe Norm, but gives him the benefit of the doubt.

We ended up hiring Norm, who became an important part of our success during his time with the company. After meeting my dad, Judy finally believed Norm's story about a daylong interview.

My dad was more than committed to the interview process. He wanted to learn everything he could about a person who was potentially joining Famous—especially a key leader. He didn't worry about time. Bringing in the wrong candidate costs more time than it takes to bring in the right one the first time. Getting to know Norm was important to my dad, no matter how long it took. It was a genuine process for him. His passion for people continues to this day and will live on forever.

Chapter 23

The Sharing of Knowledge

as told by Marc Blaushild

The first few years I worked at Famous, I often drove to the office with my father. I clearly remember the daily drive from where we lived in Cleveland to our corporate headquarters in Akron. The commute along old Route 8 took at least an hour each way, and sometimes an hour and a half during bad weather. It took even longer when construction started on the new Route 8, but that gave us plenty of time to talk. The front seat of his car is where most of my business education took place.

My dad is a very passionate speaker, and he easily gets excited talking about business situations, especially when it deals with people. I would listen intently from the passenger seat with a legal pad in my lap and pen in hand to jot down the advice he shared on the road.

One winter morning I was listening to my dad explain a marketing promotion he was charged up about. The roads were icy, with slick spots and drifting snow obscuring our path to work. I glanced out my passenger window just in time to see a truck next to us hit a patch of ice and veer toward our lane. "Look out!" I yelled, and dad turned the wheel slightly, calmly veering our car onto the median where it stuck soundly in a snowdrift.

Without missing a beat, my dad kept talking about this marketing initiative. He never even commented on the situation, like, "Wow, we almost got hit by that truck!" or, "We're stuck in the middle of the highway—what are we going to do?" He just kept talking about the business and the marketing campaign.

After five minutes, he finally took a breath, and I interjected, "Dad, I think we should walk to the Holiday Inn down the road and call a tow truck." That's how intensely focused he was on Famous. Those times together in the car—at least the times we managed to stay on the road—were the best times for me to tap into his passion and experience.

Every day, I got out of his car with a full sheet of notes listing the thoughts and ideas I wanted to try to implement from our conversation. It's hard to remember specific interactions or notes I took from the passenger seat because those lessons have become ingrained into my leadership style and decision-making process.

The main theme I internalized is that we have to take care of our people. If we take care of our people, they will take care of our customers and our customers will take care of our business.

I do remember one particular discussion we had on our morning commute: We were having an issue with a customer that owed us money. He suggested, "If you're not having luck getting ahold of this customer during the week, why don't you try to reach him on a Saturday? People are usually stressed when they're in the office. If you talk on a weekend, it may be more relaxed and casual." So, I took his advice and called this customer on Saturday, and it opened a whole new world between us. We developed a relationship that Saturday, and the next week he sent a check to settle his account. He eventually became a much larger account, and a friend, simply because we connected on a personal level outside of normal business hours at my dad's suggestion.

As much as I've learned from my father, I've had many other mentors at Famous through the years, like Bill Maxwell, Richard Newman, Frank Platz Sr., Sonny Adao, and John Kallos, to name a few. Tom Krejci was one of my first bosses when I worked at Famous during summer breaks as a kid, and he shared lessons with me that had been passed down to him through many generations of Famous associates.

"I remember when I became Cleveland branch manager," Tom says, "I was amazed because I was the youngest manager in the region, and all the fellows took me under their wings and helped me. They never looked down on me, never gave me a hard time; they were always teaching, asking how they could help and suggesting different approaches to try."

A culture of mentoring is the Famous Way. Our willingness to teach and mentor each other is like a tradition we pass down to new associates because we were all mentored when we joined the company, too. Newcomers may think they know what typically happens in a company, but it's up to the veterans to explain how and why things are different at Famous.

Dave Figuly says, "The more experienced people at Famous here have always been willing to share knowledge, explain the company history and take new people under their wing. We tell them what the company's about, what we stand for and what it means to Live The Famous Way. The way people share knowledge with new people coming in is a core part of our culture. We're not concerned that someone will take our job and think we have to keep all of our knowledge to ourselves. After all, we got it from other people, too." There's no question that we all have something to learn from everyone. It comes down to people being open-minded, wanting to teach and willing to learn.

In 2007, about 20 years after my daily commutes with my father, Brian (19 years old at the time) rode with me to his summer internship at Famous. Kevin, who was still in high school, also joined the company that summer to assist with a technology project. I learned from my dad that those father-son drives were a valuable opportunity to spend quality time together and talk about the business.

The commute was a little shorter this time around, thanks to the new Route 8; the improvements reduced our drive time to about 35 minutes each way. The parallel between the construction work on Route 8 and the improvements we had made at Famous during the same time frame intrigued me. Investments we made in our computer system, logistics network, and organizational structure allowed us to streamline our activities and grow our business, just like the improvements on Route 8 streamlined traffic to accommodate increased volume.

Personally, I didn't mind the construction delays or the bumps in the road on our drive to work. I knew that in the long-term, these changes were for the better.

Sometimes it's one step back, two steps forward. Bumps in the road are just short-term obstacles that pave the way for long-term progress.

Whether it happens in the car, the office or anywhere in between, we encourage mutually beneficial mentoring relationships throughout Famous. We ask people who have expertise to spread that knowledge for the good of our company and its long-term sustainability.

Chapter 24

Getting the Right People in the Right Roles

as told by Marc Blaushild

Sometimes it takes a while to get an associate into the right seat on the bus. Throughout the years, there have been associates at Famous who have struggled to the point where other companies would cut ties with them. Maybe they didn't work well with their manager or struggled with a certain skill required for their role. Fortunately, we have leaders who have done an incredible job of getting those people into roles that fit their skill-set, so they could thrive and become stars.

My grandfather and my father both had an incredible ability move an associate into the right position if they weren't performing well in their current role. The easiest people to let go are the obvious bad apples—the people with bad attitudes, or those who are obvious liabilities to the business. However, it isn't as easy to recognize the potential in someone who's struggling and have the vision to move them into a role where they'll be happy and succeed. If associates share our Core Values, Live The Famous Way and are smart, it's up to us to find the position where they can add the most value to the team.

To make those moves, you need a deep understanding of a person's skills, interests and potential, combined with knowing what it takes to succeed in various roles throughout the company.

We make sure managers are taking the time to know their people through their monthly "1-2-1s". 1-2-1s are closed-door meetings between managers and their direct reports. We require every manager to have 1-2-1 meetings with their direct reports every month to get a better understanding of their people's perspectives, review performance and get clear on mutual expectations. We have a form that guides the conversation with questions like:

1. What is the most important thing you want to discuss today?
2. What are the top priorities, projects, or activities you're focused on?
3. As your manager, should I be doing anything differently?
4. Do you need more training/development? If so, in what areas?

This process can be extremely effective for discussing business opportunities, areas of improvement for the business, and individual career/development opportunities that may not come up during normal, everyday conversations.

"Marc learned about these 1-2-1 meetings in his Vistage Group and brought that idea to the Leadership team," says John Palermo. "He told us, 'I want us all to have formal, scheduled one-on-one meetings with our direct reports once every month.' I was thinking, 'Well, I already talk to my guys almost every day, so what are we going to talk about for another hour?'

But I was wrong. When we set aside time, just me and the associate, we can talk about the business uninterrupted; priorities, challenges, roadblocks, resources, training needs, or other issues. More importantly, we get to know one another on a more personal level. I get to know what really drives them because we all love Famous, but not as much as we love our families, our children and the things that are most important to us. When you get to understand how they tick internally, then you really get to know them.

In the beginning when Marc brought it up, I thought, 'Another one of these fads.' But now I'm the biggest proponent for 1-2-1 meetings in the company. They are especially important to the people who don't have years of experience because they can bounce around ideas or discuss their experiences. It's valuable to have help as you feel your way through situations. I learn a lot through them too, since they're in the field closest to our associates and customers.

I think if I don't do 1-2-1s, I'm failing the associate. No matter where you are, it's everyone's responsibility to teach every associate what they need to learn and grow in the business. Watching a person grow personally and professionally is fulfilling. That does my soul good because it means either I, or someone else on our team, has helped develop that individual."

While career growth is something we celebrate, one thing we don't want to promote is a culture where individuals constantly think about their next career move rather than performing at a high level in their current role for the betterment of the company. In addition, while we want to develop our own and promote from within, we need steady, reliable performers who do their job well, are happy in their role and can help develop others. We don't push associates too hard to pursue development opportunities if their current job makes them happy. As John Palermo says:

"There was a truck driver who worked with us when I was running the Akron branch who I felt would be a great salesperson. So, I said, 'Lloyd, I think you'd be great in the Counter Sales role. I'd like you to spend time at the Counter, so you can get exposed to some products, and we can start a career path for you.'

'No, John,' he'd say. 'I'm not interested.'

This went on for about five or six months, and I kept trying different approaches to bring him over to sales. He finally looked at me and said, 'John, what I want to do in life is drive truck because I love driving truck.'

At that point, this became a learning experience for me. I said, 'Okay. You know what you're going to do for the team, Lloyd? Drive truck.' And he was great at it because that's what he loved to do. My goal then became helping Lloyd to be the best truck driver he could be."

Some people fit their current roles perfectly, and others have more potential to shine in different positions. Most people enjoy the roles they're in and they feel like they're contributing to our success best in that role. Others are looking for other opportunities to grow into different roles and we want to provide those opportunities as they became available.

"I've heard stories about people who were struggling 20 years ago, and instead of getting rid of them, we worked with them and moved them around to different roles," Brian says. "It might take a few different positions, but eventually they find a role in which they flourish, and 20 years later they're one of the best we have. If people fit the Core Values, live the Fundamentals and have a skill-set to bring to the team, we're committed to helping them find the right seat on the bus, even when most companies would rather part ways."

Chapter 25

Teamwork in Tough Times
as told by Marc Blaushild

Most years have been fruitful at Famous, where we're building momentum, having fun and progressing as a company. But in business and life, it's not always smooth sailing. Sometimes obstacles are uncontrollable external factors or are self-induced through internal challenges. The difficult times are when successful teams realize that the only option is to work together and take care of one another to survive.

Recent economic recessions also happened to coincide with significant internal changes at Famous. Shortly after we reorganized the business, opened the Central Distribution Center and computerized our entire operation, we were battling against the economic conditions. The tough times compounded into a perfect storm of challenges. John Palermo remembers:

"We'd already struggled through a difficult fourth quarter in 2008. The US economy and housing market crashed, and it was a tough year for sales. New housing starts were off 75 percent and our commodity inventory values, especially steel, dropped over 50 percent. As a management team, we all shared in that pain. The Executive Leadership Team members all took pay cuts. There wasn't much finger pointing. Our attitude was that this is our problem to solve together."

As the challenges piled up, our people pulled together. We didn't have to ask people to work longer hours or practice blameless problem-solving with each other. Everybody just stepped up. They knew what we had to accomplish, and they worked through it together.

At Heating and Cooling Products (HCP), a Famous Enterprises company that's run independently from Famous Supply, we faced an even more difficult challenge. We had a person working full-time buying steel coils that HCP used to make furnace pipe, duct and fittings. He proposed the idea of selling coils to other manufacturers in addition to using them to make our own products.

We're always open to ideas from our associates who see opportunities in the marketplace, so we gave him the go-ahead. We brought in some inventory and sold it, and sales grew from $2 million to $8 million during the first two years. The third year, it grew to nearly $20 million.

We had a meeting to discuss this segment of the business, and I'll never forget what he asked me: "How much business do you want to do next year? $30 million? $40? $50?" Cautious of growing too fast, we went for $30 million in sales. To get there, we needed to buy more inventory.

Steel pricing was at its peak. We gave him the go-ahead to place purchase orders for a five-month supply. Soon after he placed the order, the stock market crashed. Housing went from 2 million new homes to under 500,000. Most sheet metal pipe, duct and fittings go into new construction, and we watched the market drop 75 percent. The pricing of the inventory we had just purchased was slashed by more than 60 percent.

When we place a purchase order, we honor our commitment. We spent about six months negotiating with our supplier, and our CFO and I flew out to the West Coast to meet with them face-to-face. Because we communicated, built trust and addressed the issue directly, we worked together toward a mutually beneficial resolution. It took about a year to work through the process, but because we were transparent and forthcoming, our relationship with this supplier grew stronger.

Ultimately, we decided not to continue in the steel brokerage business anymore, choosing rather to stay focused within our core distribution and manufacturing business. We eventually used some of our supply of steel coil and sold some at a huge loss after write-downs. Ultimately, it turned into cash we could invest in other areas.

Even though we took a big hit on the chin, we did what we said we would do and maintained our relationship with the supplier who remains an important business partner today.

We learned our lessons: to temper our enthusiasm when things look too good to be true and to practice greater due diligence in big investments. We also had to rely on our partners for help when the factors impacting our business were out of our control. That teamwork, trust and communication isn't always common in every industry. Most distribution companies have similar processes for buying, pricing, storing, and delivering products. But culturally, the way people work through difficult issues is important. We're proud of the fact that we work together when issues come up, and our customers and suppliers notice it.

"Famous associates view themselves as part of a team, and we get great satisfaction from helping the overall team succeed," says Brady Rubin, Director of Plumbing Products. "You can see that every day, in every associate—from Counter Sales associates to Truck Drivers to the Warehouse Manager. We're a true team with great synergy."

What difference does great teamwork make? Look at the 2014 Ryder Cup, an international golf tournament where America's best golfers play against Europe's best. Our captain was a legendary player and the American coach who took a command-and-control approach to running the team. It was his way or the highway. According to various accounts, he didn't listen to his players. As a result, they weren't in the best position for their strengths to shine. The European coach took a more holistic approach. He listened to his players and used that communication and trust to build develop a strategy. They were a team. They didn't win every match, but they improved enough throughout the course of three days of golf to win it and keep the prized Ryder Cup for the third straight time.

That's the approach we prefer to take. Authoritative, command-and-control management may have worked 40 years ago. But now, and in the future, it's the collaborative teams that win. We've found that teamwork simply makes the work more fun. People feel better about their work when they feel like they can influence decisions and understand "the Why" behind them. When the whole team contributes to the win, the celebration is genuinely better.

CONTINUOUS IMPROVEMENT

Chapter 26

Celebrating 75 Years
as told by Marc Blaushild

During the difficult times of the early 2000s, we made investments to build a strong team and put infrastructure and systems in place that would benefit us long-term. Beyond the recession, we saw a horizon of opportunities to grow our market share and expand our business. We'd made it through some of the toughest market conditions and biggest changes our company had ever endured. Through wars, depressions, recessions, and other economic crises, Famous not only survived, but grew and prospered. Although the hard times were far from over our team deserved a celebration for making it this far. Early in my career I went to a trade show in Chicago where a speaker said there are two things people want in a job. One is to work on challenging and interesting things—and we'd definitely been through challenges. The other is to be recognized for their accomplishments, and we had decades' worth of celebrating to do.

With our 75th anniversary approaching in 2008, we planned our biggest party yet. We saw it as an investment worth making because we felt it was important to celebrate together and reinforce our Famous Family as we looked to the future.

We called it our Renaissance, which by definition, means rebirth and revival. It was a fitting name because as we emerged from our biggest challenges we were being reborn as an organization. The 75th anniversary was a time to honor and celebrate the heritage and strong foundation we'd built and galvanize our team around the opportunities that were ahead. We knew our current position would not be possible without the leaders and associates who came before us and worked so hard. We also knew our company always had a special culture with special people who shared the values that drove our decisions. But we had never defined these values in writing. Our renaissance was the perfect time to do it.

Six months before our big anniversary, we set out to determine what our Core Values really were. At the same time, we conducted in-depth strategy sessions, break-out groups and off-site meetings. We had to identify our Core Values, vision, strategy, and goals as a company. We evaluated our products, customer segments, markets, and our competitors to assess where we were and where we wanted to go.

Our strategy had transformed throughout the years, and our culture had slowly shifted along with it. However, our values were the constant, unwavering fiber of our being. We had to focus on the ones that stood the test of time that we saw reflected through every generation of Famous. They would have to be as important in the 2030s as they were in the 1930s. That process required careful consideration.

After many meetings, discussions, ideas, and reflections, we came to agreement on five foundational Core Values. These values encompass the most important aspects of our organization: Family, Trust, Communication, Teamwork and Continuous Improvement. My father says:

"We spent a lot of time discussing our Core Values. It turned out to be worth it because we put it in a form that's easier for people to see and recognize. If a person is with us 30 years, they could already feel the Core Values because they've experienced it. But when you hire in new people, you need to communicate the values of your company to find the right fit. I'm 100 percent comfortable with how we state our Core Values today and I'm sure my dad, Hyman, would be, too. I think he would take exceptional pride to see what we've done."

Appropriately, we selected the Renaissance Hotel in Cleveland as the site of our Renaissance celebration in April 2008. We invited our top 75 customers, our top 75 suppliers, and all of our associates to the event. Because we didn't have room to accommodate everyone, we also took the party on the road by having appreciation events for customers, suppliers and associates at each of our branches leading up to the main event that summer.

Over 1,200 members of the Famous Family joined us in downtown Cleveland for the weekend-long event, full of recognizing associates who'd contributed to our success throughout the years.

At the main event dinner that Saturday night, we debuted a short film featuring stories from my father, me and other long-time associates about our rich history. We also presented our Core Values, new corporate goals, plans and vision so everyone could hear the same message from us at once. Several Senior and Regional Managers spoke to explain key objectives for their respective areas of responsibility. Our motivational keynote speaker was Mike Eruzione, captain of the 1980 USA Olympic hockey team and gold medalist. We also brought in guest speakers to stimulate creative thinking. Two bands played throughout the weekend, so people could relax, dance and have fun with their Famous Family.

The purpose of this two-day event was to celebrate and communicate. We wanted everyone leaving that weekend to be on the same page with our Core Values, vision, plans, and goals. We wanted our associates to feel like an integral part of the company's past and future accomplishments. It was to show people we care about them deeply, to motivate each one as an important part of our team and to let them know how we would share in our team success. I envisioned how our 75th anniversary weekend would unfold, but it exceeded my wildest expectations. It was a special and memorable time for all of us, mostly because we shared it together as one Famous Family.

Recapping the event in the quarterly company newsletter afterward I wrote:

Although we have endured the test of time as an organization since 1933, we are only just beginning our rebirth. We are still learning in our journey toward achieving our vision to be a great company. We must always value our company's heritage. Those who came before us worked so hard to provide us with incredible opportunities. But we can nev-

er get complacent. We must think with the curiosity and creativity of a child. We must be nimble and not get caught in the proverbial trap of saying, 'This is the way we have always done it,' because it may not be the best way in current times.

We must work together as a team, so we continue to improve. We need to respect the generations before us, their wisdom and experience, and blend what we know with new and innovative ideas we learn to better serve our customers. Thanks to those who preceded our current team, we have a solid foundation to build Famous Enterprises to greater heights.

However, we must be humble and continually ask ourselves: 'Are we willing to listen to new ideas and learn from others, regardless of their age or experience?' It doesn't matter if you're a Driver or a Director; a great idea is a great idea. We need to value everyone's thoughts and opinions. I challenge you to ask: Are we all listening to our coworkers, suppliers and customers? Are we stuck in our ways, or thinking outside the box?

Today, just like during the Renaissance Era 600 years ago, there is an art to learning. It starts with questioning the status quo by asking 'why?' or 'what if?' questions. Think back to what it was like when the Renaissance Hotel was built in Cleveland in 1918. A huge investment was made to build a world-class hotel. When they opened for business, they needed to have a smart, well-trained team in place to be successful. Fast-forward almost a century; the Renaissance invested in new technology, wiring, sound, lighting, and video equipment to create a new and exciting experience in the ballroom for customers. They renovated their rooms, probably multiple times. This was all achieved by people who challenged the status-quo. As an organization, we need to take the same approach to learning from one another. We need to blend the old wisdom with new knowledge.

Chapter 27

Back to Basics

as told by Marc Blaushild

After our 75th anniversary, Famous moved forward through some of the most trying times our company had ever faced. I stressed to our team that we couldn't become complacent or rest our laurels. We had to keep working as a cohesive team to continue serving our customers through the Great Recession.

As the economy fluctuates and the industry advances, there's a tendency to over complicate business. When it comes to servicing our customers, it's critical we keep things simple and continue mastering the basics.

There wasn't a lot of complexity in how Hyman Blaushild ran the business when it began. He focused on the basics of giving contractors good service. He knew customers had three main questions: "Do you have it? How much is it? When can I get it?" He and the team worked to ensure we could answer these three simple questions and give customers solutions they needed.

This philosophy remains true today. If we've got the products our customers need in stock, can provide them when and where they need, at a fair and competitive price, without damaging it, we're confident we'll be our customers' preferred supplier. Our business boils down to the fundamental blocking and tackling, and that's what Famous has focused on since the beginning.

Technology has certainly changed the game. Today, customers expect more than when my grandfather started Famous. Until just a few decades ago, they didn't mind the handwritten orders or the time it took to get the right products to them. Now, customers expect products and information to travel at the speed of technology, with added efficiencies and conveniences along the way.

As we strive to improve the efficiency of each process involved in serving our customer, we get closer to our ultimate goal of providing world-class operational excellence. In the words of Kevin:

"We understand that the only way we can keep customers for life is by giving them the best service. However, service is a word that's constantly evolving, because what might have been important to the customer 10 years ago, or even five years ago, differs from what will be important to them today, or five years from today. We have to keep improving."

That doesn't always require drastic changes like restructuring our entire operation. More often, it's the simple, little things that can make us more effective. We define continuous improvement at Famous as doing anything we can a little better each day. The improvements add up to doing things a lot better over the long-term. For us, that means focusing on the details of execution; mastering the Perfect Order from start to finish.

Whether massive or minor, the changes we've rolled out at Famous spur from our Core Value of Continuous Improvement. Through Trust, Communication, and Teamwork, we've built a culture that encourages associates to keep asking questions and sharing ideas. A big part of that is creating a culture where ideas that fail are viewed stepping stones on the path to finding the right solution. We're more concerned with someone staying silent and content with status quo than suggesting ideas that don't end up working.

If we're complacent and always accept things as they are, we'll end up in trouble. We have to always keep an open mind and open everything up to the exploration of continuous improvement.

As we're constantly pushing toward emerging technologies and new ways of serving our customers, we must remember that newer is not better for everyone.

We have to be mindful of our underlying purpose, which is to Build Meaningful Relationships for Life, and all customers are unique. A conversation I had with one of our customers at a recent Expo illustrates this perfectly.

I ran into Tony, a customer for 30 years, in our technology services area. I asked him if he was familiar with our e-commerce services like our new mobile app. He chuckled and replied that technology wasn't for him. I asked why he felt that way, and he pulled an ancient flip phone out of his front shirt pocket. He said, "this is all I need to deal with my customers; a phone to talk to them." Even more important, he said, was face-to-face contact. As long as he's been in business, he's never advertised. Through word-of-mouth and face-to-face interaction, he's as busy as he could be. His focus was service, not new technology.

I continued asking why he was against looking at new technologies if they could improve his service. He told me his life story; he was one of eight children, and his father was a boxer. A boxing injury led his dad to a railroad job where he made 15 cents an hour. His father worked hard to support the family while imparting the value of building face-to-face, personal relationships. That's how Tony lived his life and ran his business, and he felt as strongly about his approach as I felt about our technology.

This conversation helped me remember that all customers have unique wants and needs. No matter how much we believe in what we're selling, what we need to do is listen to our customers and align with the way they want to do business with Famous. Some want to call an Inside Sales rep, others prefer coming into a branch, while some may want to meet with an Outside Sales rep in their office. Now, an increasing number prefer to order online and have their product delivered with minimal human interaction. People want to do business with us different ways at different times, and what works best for them is best for Famous. When our goal is to meet the customer's specific wants and needs, we can be flexible to deliver the best experience for them. No matter how the world changes, the same questions remain: "Do you have it? How much is it? When can I get it?"

Chapter 28

Famous University
as told by Marc Blaushild

Many good companies listen to feedback from their associates, customers and vendors to tune into the market and keep pace with the industry. We're not only thinking about what our partners need to be successful today. We're thinking ahead to what they will need, before they even know they need it. As Wayne Gretzky said, "You don't skate to where the puck is. You skate to where it will be." Brent Grover, an original member of our Famous Advisory Board explains:

"I've worked with companies where the leaders are living in the past, and that's scary. I've worked with companies where the leaders are living in the present, and they tend to execute well. Famous looks deep in the future, and Marc is always planning the next move. If the next generation can make that vision real and continue looking forward, success will continue. I already see and sense that's happening with Brian and Kevin. They're helping their customers solve problems they don't even have yet, and that type of anticipation is rare."

Stay ahead of our customers' future needs, we've prioritized training future generations (both associates and customers) to prepare them for what's coming next.

Education and training have always been an integral part of the fabric of Famous. My father and grandfather were passionate about providing development opportunities for our growing team.

"We strongly emphasized education, both technical and otherwise," my dad says. "I rarely turned down anyone who wanted to go to a seminar or take a class, and my dad hardly did, either. If someone wanted to go to an air conditioning school for a week, we felt the investment in education would provide long-term return that was worth being short-handed for a few days."

We've always seen value in training our people and sharing knowledge, so the next step was to build a platform where that training could happen consistently. In my five-year crystal ball, I wrote about the development of Famous University, a platform for lifelong learning in our organization. Fortunately, Famous University became more than that, but we still have a long way to go.

Training our own associates is still integral to our approach. I am absolutely convinced that all companies need to commit more resources to learning, development and coaching. The winning companies will be the ones that provide the most quality development opportunities to their people. That might mean taking people out of revenue-generating jobs for hours or days at a time to go through training. The best, world-class companies are the ones willing to invest in education that builds long-term benefits.

Famous University officially opened in 2007 as an internal resource to educate associates on our vision and the technical skills they needed to achieve our collective goals. It quickly evolved into something bigger as many of our customers were just as passionate about receiving similar training to improve their organizations. In line with our commitment to serve and make them better, we opened enrollment to customers.

Many of our customers require continuing education course hours every year to keep their certifications, so most of our technical courses are certified by the state of Ohio. Most of our HVAC classes are also certified by North American Technician Excellence (NATE). However, the point of the program is not merely to meet quotas for certification. Over time, we developed an innovative curriculum to provide industry professionals with courses, hands-on workshops, webinars, seminars, and training materials intended to raise the standards for the fields we serve.

Courses cover everything from the basic to highly specific technical topics, such as servicing modulating furnaces and troubleshooting water heater control systems. We also offer general business classes covering sales and marketing, customer service, accounting, and QuickBooks for contractors.

When they're not training, our on-staff instructors assist customers with technical support and troubleshooting, so they're a constant resource whether a class is in session or not. We've also developed a "Build A Tech" program where our instructors take a customer's newest field techs through a rigorous training program for nine months to help get them ready to work in the field.

The main training centers for Famous University are in our Central Distribution Center and our corporate headquarters. Traditionally, customers knew Famous as their local branch. Many of them don't realize the resources available to them until they visit our CDC or headquarters for the first time. That's why we based Famous University within our Central Distribution Center—as an invitation for customers to visit our facilities and see more of Famous.

Famous University has been successful in training customers and associates, especially when our industry needs to react to widespread change. Bruce Carnevale, from Bradford White, explains:

> "In 2015, the water heater industry went through the biggest product change we've ever seen. The Department of Energy changed regulations, and we needed to react. Famous was at the forefront of training our mutual customers and helping them through this transition. From formal training programs at Famous University to informal education during everyday business, this was a big help to us as a manufacturer. It's very frustrating when we work on our end to communicate through the channel, and then we meet a contractor or a builder who hasn't heard the message. We don't find that with Famous' customers. They provide the training and put people in place who are experts to take ownership of supplier product lines. They're a true partner in taking information through the channel all the way to the contractor."

In the past, some would say distributors simply moved the boxes. But training customers how to use the products and offering support for them adds value beyond the product itself to make our customers more successful.

"One of the best legacies we leave is through education and continued support of the industries we're a part of," says Elio Andretta, Director of HVAC Products. "We've made a lot of investments in training and continued education to our customers. Trust me, that's not a big money-making thing. It's a contribution and commitment to the industry that you don't see with a lot of other organizations."

Chapter 29

Continuous Improvement Mindset
as told by Marc Blaushild

In the late 1990s our transformation was about survival. We had to move to a computer system to keep up with competitors. Now, we're taking our technology to the next level, not to keep pace, but to set the pace for our industry. The addition of our Central Distribution Center (and the software that drives it) was a game changer. We built the facility around a system that virtualized our warehouse and the inventory in it. Throughout several years, we slowly integrated the rest of our branches into the ERP to bring our warehouses together into one integrated system. Once that happened, we took the next step to enable our customers to interact with our system online.

Our e-commerce business has grown exponentially since it launched. Our customers now place more than $30 million in sales annually online. It's been growing about 25 percent per year, and our mobile app for smartphones and iPads is growing even faster. Adopting these new technologies doesn't mean we lose the personal touch of face-to-face communication that our company was founded upon. We see technology as a way to enhance, not replace, the personal relationships with have with our customers.

With our mobile e-commerce platform, customers have access to inventory availability, their pricing, their account balance, and can place orders. Our pickers receive those tickets and immediately fulfill customer orders. Product ships the next day, and sometimes the same day, to the customer's local branch for pick-up, or directly to their shop or job site. When the order ships, it posts to the customer's account and an invoice automatically generates. This process still amazes me when I think back to the week it used to take for this entire process to happen manually.

We've implemented delivery software to alert customers when their delivery is coming. When we're routing our trucks at 5 a.m., we text or email notifications to let customers know exactly when they can expect their delivery. If the truck is running early or late, the customer will receive an updated time of arrival. The software then sends a message confirming when the product was delivered and who signed for it. With just a few keystrokes, a customer can review the manifest for the delivery, which allows them to better manage their installation and labor crews.

Previously, if customers had returns or warranty issues, they went to their local branch for help. It might have taken a while for the credit to post to their account, and while we often received the warranty credits we submitted, we didn't have a consistent process across the company. Once the Central Distribution Center was up and running, it made sense to centralize and expedite the way we handled warranties, so we established our Central Warranty Team.

Today, we're capturing more data and metrics than ever to analyze our day-to-day operations, so we can better serve our customers. This is how we identify root causes of issues and opportunities to keep getting better and better.

BRANCH MAKEOVERS

While the Central Distribution Center is an obvious example of our commitment to continuous improvement, we take the same approach inside every branch and showroom. Over the past five years we've been updating and remodeling the inside of every branch counters in our company to ensure customers have an outstanding experience with Famous.

When Famous Supply of Sandusky moved across town into a new building in early 2005, our quarterly newsletter showcased pictures of the clean, renovated counter with more product merchandising than we typically did at that time. That kicked off a counter makeover contest challenging each branch to submit before-

and-after photos of their improvements.

The contest prompted our team in Toledo to renovate an old office next to their counter. They looked at this rarely used storage room as a new opportunity to serve customers better. They knocked out the display window and add a counter top in its place to create an Express Will Call counter. The office has a door that opens to the front dock where customers can pull in through the garage doors and park for fast loading.

Associates pulled and prepared more orders before customers arrived at the branch. Within just a few months, half of Famous Toledo's counter business was using the Express Will Call, and they received compliments from customers who were getting to their jobs more quickly. We want customers who call ahead to be in and out with their orders in under a minute - time is critical for their profitability.

After the contest we gave awards for the most improved and best overall counters. But every branch that made improvements were winners because they were providing customers a better shopping experience.

Although that contest ended some years ago, we've continued doing large scale renovations in every branch throughout the company. "When customers come to our branches, we want to make sure they're having a great experience," says John Palermo. "We want all of our counters to have a consistent look and feel, while also giving branches freedom to pick which products they want to display for their unique market."

Tom Krejci was with Famous for 45 years in a variety of roles. As Director of Marketing, then Director of Special Projects, he spent years working with branches to make the counters consistently attractive and effective. Tom says:

"Every month when Marc has his conference call, he tells people, 'We want to increase our sales per invoice.' Guess where that's easiest to do? At the counter. So, I go out to all the stores and evaluate how we can improve them while making smart investments. We try to move stuff in and out—more popular products that are spur-of-the-moment, point-of-purchase types of products. We've tried things like windshield washer fluid, because if a customer doesn't have the chance to stop at a gas station, they can pick it up from us at a competitive price. We also brought in shovels for plumbers at two branches to test the response.

Our product mix is more consistent now, but, we've expanded our horizons of what we offer at the counters. I encourage our team to be creative and always try to think of new products we can sell at the counters. If it makes sense for the customer base and the company, our attitude is, 'let's try it.'

That's a positive thing about the company. No one ever said to me, 'Hey Tom, you're nuts. What are you doing?' They say, 'Let's be innovative.' You won't know what will work until you try. People have fun trying something new at the counter after I leave. They have the liberty to explore new ways to grow their business. If you're coming up with ways to expand your business and get more customers, nobody would ever question that. We've sold millions of dollars of generators in recent years because someone realized there was a market for it and spoke up.

I'm happy to say our sales growth has been strong at the counters because of the people around the company simply trying new things. We're improving the counters drastically. When associates see that the company is putting money back into their local branch it builds morale. That's exciting for an old guy like me."

The physical changes inside branches are a microcosm for how our business is constantly improving. We combine our knowledge of customers with the efficiencies of scalable processes, and never stop asking "How can we be better?"

Our Cleveland East location on Woodland Avenue was the first Famous location. My father used to walk there after school to meet his dad who sat in an office surrounded by his collection of miniature liquor bottles. In the summer of 2015, we carefully packed up my grandfather's bottle collection for the move to our new headquarters, and completely modernized the remaining warehouse facility. We opened thousands of square feet, added new lighting and displays, and gave the warehouse a fresh coat of paint. We refreshed the whole environment that gave us our start. This extra space allowed us to bring in plumbing inventory and promote building products. This was a location better known for HVAC since 1933.

It's the same building with the same foundation. We're running the same business and serving an expanded customer base. We look a little sharper and do things a little better to make the whole customer experience more enjoyable.

Chapter 30

Moving Out of the Castle

as told by Marc

For 35 years, our corporate headquarters ("The Castle") was a novelty for associates, customers and vendors. The Castle was built in 1895 for the Werner Printing & Lithograph Co., which produced encyclopedias and dictionaries decades before Famous bought the building. The storied building was a fitting representation of Famous. The beautiful red bricks, elegant crown molding and charm represented our strong foundation, creativity and unique culture. However, the challenges of operating a business out of The Castle also represented the challenges Famous faced in the 1980s.

First, the building's disjointed layout of four floors. Each had numerous offices and kept our team separated. Our Customer Support Center was located in another building down the street and created even greater barriers toward communication and teamwork. By the 2010s, the major repairs needed to keep the building operational continued to increase. So just as we became a team through our ERP system, revamped organizational structure and integrated distribution network, we needed to physically come together at the corporate level to facilitate the collaboration we so often preached. We needed a new facility if we wanted to grow and prosper.

We identified a building in Akron, Ohio, about 10 minutes away from The Castle, that was the perfect fit. Our vision was to bring corporate functions and our

Customer Support Center under one roof. We designed a layout that would ensure collaboration, so we could work on the business and best serve customers.

After nearly a year of construction, we moved into our new Corporate Headquarters in August 2015. The purpose of our move into a new, modern facility was not to have a fancy place to work. While we wanted to give our associates a comfortable place to do their jobs, the foremost need was for increased face-to-face collaboration. Breaking down the physical barriers that impede communication goes a long way.

We merged what were previously five separate floors of fragmented work spaces into two floors of open architecture. This included nine conference rooms, a large training room and a beautiful café. We also proudly put our history on display. We turned a picture from my grandfather's contracting days into wallpaper for our lobby. We crafted a wall of the conference room nearest the lobby out of my grandfather's miniature liquor bottle collection. A timeline of significant events in the company's history scales the entrance hallway.

This change wasn't met without concern from some of our people. Just like the decision to open our Central Distribution Center in 2005, some associates weren't sure it would work. Many people had been working in the same office for years and weren't used to being in an open environment.

Not only did our associates adjust; they thrived. Now, there isn't a single person in our building who would go back to the old Castle or Customer Support Center. John Palermo said, "Many people were worried about the change. You have folks who get used to working a certain way for so many years and it's very comfortable. But Marc did a great job explaining why we needed to make a change and illustrating the benefits it would give to the company and our customers. There isn't an associate in our headquarters that doesn't love being in that facility."

Throughout the years, we've gone through so many changes. Most have been positive. The constant is the resilience of our associates and their ability to embrace change. This was just another change. Our people, as always, adapted, evolved and became stronger along the way.

Chapter 31

Giving Back
as told by Marc Blaushild

As we reflect on the company's success and our own personal blessings throughout the years, we realize there are many who are less fortunate than ourselves. In the spirit of caring for our extended Famous Family and the communities we serve, Famous is committed to giving back to those in need.

Famous partnered with The Make-A-Wish® Foundation in the early 2000s to raise money through activities like golf outings and raffles and provide personal involvement from the entire Famous Family.

The first child we sponsored was a young girl near Lorain, Ohio who wished for her own swing set. Instead of just sending money, Famous brought about 20 volunteers to her home to build it for her. Our handy associates, customers and suppliers pitched in to build her an incredible swing set, and she was thrilled.

We've raised more than $200,000 for over 30 kids through The Make-A-Wish Foundation, partnering with our supplier, Luxaire, to bring these wishes to life. We have a Make-A-Wish Wall of Fame in the cafe in our headquarters featuring framed pictures of the children we've sponsored through this program. Our customers also get involved, making donations and attending the parties we host for the children. We often partner with other customers and suppliers to donate our time and services to families in need. In 2009, we teamed up with Ollinger Plumbing and Heating to provide an HVAC makeover for a family in the Ollinger's hometown of Erie, Pa. Famous donated the materials and the Ollinger team volunteered labor to replace the family's HVAC system. Just imagine all those plumbers, framers, electricians, and contractors working around each other in a 2,000-square-foot home at 3 a.m. It was a heartwarming experience for us all.

We also look to our associates for ideas for the organizations we support. For example, Brian came up with an idea for a fundraiser in 2013. He suggested making bright pink camouflage T-shirts (a color we rarely see inside our branches) to sell during October for Breast Cancer Awareness Month and donate the proceeds to breast cancer research.

One of our suppliers, Wincore Windows, partnered with us to create these "Tough Enough to Wear Pink" T-shirts. That month we sold over 600 T-shirts and had a company-wide pink shirt day where we all wore them to work. About half of our branches added bake sales, raffles and other fundraisers to support the Susan G. Komen Foundation.

Soon after Kevin, joined the company, we were on a customer appreciation trip in Jamaica when he suggested we visit a local orphanage as an excursion. He borrowed the idea from a plumbing wholesaler we knew in Wisconsin. Some of our customers had done similar types of mission or charity work, so they jumped at the idea. We stopped by a local store and bought toys, books, games, blankets, and food for the kids.

We delivered all of this to the Robin's Nest orphanage in Jamaica and spent some time meeting the children there. This visit was an eye-opening experience that made a positive impact on all of us. After our visit we continued to think about these kids and their incredibly selfless caregivers. Instead of just bringing back stories and slideshows from our trip, we brought the cause back with us. Famous offered to match donations as we raised additional money from our associates, customers and suppliers so we could send more support to those children.

This captured the hearts of the Famous Family as we received an outpouring of positive feedback from everyone who wanted to do it again the next year. As a result, the orphanage trip became a staple on our customer getaways. It has become a unique and meaningful way to further strengthen the Famous Family by giving back for the good of the greater community. To support upgrades to the facilities, we cumulatively raised more than $30,000 for the orphanages we visited in 2015 and 2016 and raised more than $50,000 in 2017 alone.

It's fairly easy to get our associates, customers and suppliers involved in these causes; all we have to do is tell them about it. The exceptional people we work with are the type of individuals who will give you the shirt off their back or pull over to the side of the road to help you with a flat tire in the middle of a snowstorm. They're honorable, giving, high-character people. When something needs to be done to help others, they naturally step up and do it.

The most recent philanthropic effort we've begun is to donate proceeds of the sales of our private label brands. We give a portion of sales of our Stream33, Bright33, Craft33, and Breeze33 products to the global water crisis, and hunger and shelter causes in our local communities. This initiative could end up being our most impactful yet.

We are extremely proud of the ways our company, our associates, customers and suppliers give back. In my office, among the many photos of my family, is a picture of a little boy writing the words on a chalkboard: "Giving Adds Up." It's a constant reminder to me, and hopefully all who see it, to always be looking for ways to give back. It feels good to give, and more importantly, it's the right thing to do.

Chapter 32

No Conclusion
as told by Marc Blaushild

I wrote in the conclusion of my five-year crystal ball prediction, "There is no conclusion. We are on a journey to develop and continuously improve individually, as a company and as a team. There is so much more to accomplish. There are dozens of other opportunities, issues and areas to address, but our priorities are clear with our Core Values and 40 Fundamentals." We want to improve the company and make each year stronger in terms of growth, sales and profitability.

Individual improvement is just as important to us. We want each associate to wake up and say, "How can I be better today than I was yesterday? How can I be better this year than I was last year?" Whether they're making deliveries to customers, loading trucks, picking product, buying, selling, serving customers at the counter, in the showroom, or in other support functions; we want them to push themselves to get better to drive the company forward collectively.

We've come a long way. We've survived economic crises and change, and grown and prospered because:

- We're aligned by our Core Values of Family, Trust, Communication, Teamwork, and Continuous Improvement, and practice our 40 Fundamentals
- We truly value all of our associates and invest in their learning, training and development

- We believe in our special Famous culture, our Famous Family and the Famous Way we serve each other, our valued customers and our key suppliers
- We know our most important priorities and why we must execute our Game Plan
- We understand how important it is to Build Meaningful Relationships for Life. We are continually striving to become a great company and share in our success.

And what does that success mean to Famous?

Brian Blaushild: Our vision is to be a great company. Our purpose is to Build Meaningful Relationships for Life. We understand that the only way we can keep customers for life is by giving them the best service we can, every moment of the day. The goal is to keep improving and get better at what we're doing. I'm not enamored with the numbers, whether it's sales or how many stores we have. As long as we get the right people who commit to making the company better, we won't fall short of our goal.

Kevin Blaushild: Success means our people are living the Fundamentals. If we're doing right by each other, our customers and suppliers, executing our game plan to operate a profitable business and innovating, we're successful.

Marc Blaushild: In line with our fifth core value of Continuous Improvement, our goal is to continue to grow the top- and bottom-line every year. As long as we continue to grow and share our success with our people, they'll understand that we're investing in them and the company, and our people will take care of customers to perpetuate our legacy. When I think about where we are as a company, where we've been and where we're going, it's exciting because our future is bright. We respect our heritage and our tradition, and work to innovate and evolve. It's all about our people. Our people care and they're working as a team, and that makes it all worthwhile.

The only way we can benefit over a long period of time is by producing positive results every day we come to work. We have to execute the blocking-and-tackling to win the game we're playing, knowing that the ultimate goal is to win the Super Bowl. Not a division championship, not a conference title, not the AFC or NFC title—the Super Bowl!

Because our sights are ultimately set on team goals that extend decades into the future, our success depends on the Famous Family working together as a team to be stronger than any one of us alone. The company can only win when the whole team wins. We've structured our business so that when the team wins, the players all share in its success.

What always strikes me when I walk through a branch and chat with associates is the way our people help each other. We have some people who are very experienced and have spent most of their lives at Famous, or in our industry. We also have people who have far less experience and are newer to the industry. Regardless of experience or position, we all work together as a team, from the branch management to the warehouse, from administrative support to sales. It always circles back to living the Fundamentals that bring our Core Values to life: supporting each other like Family, building Trust with one another, working as a Team, and Communicating openly to Continuously Improve.

Many years from now, as my sons and all other associates will walk through future branches of Famous. If they're struck by the same feeling that comes from watching our team work together to grow and improve, we will have been successful.